Outdoor Gas Griddle

Cookbook

Prepare a Bliss for Your Tastebuds with loads of Delicious & Easy Recipes. Sneak into the Top Chefs Secrets & Instantly Become Your Friends' & Family's Favorite Chef!

by

DANIEL SCOTT

Table of Contents

Game Day Recipes.............................98

Appetizer Recipes.............................103

Dessert Recipes 109

Introduction

Traditional griddles employ flat surfaces such as stones and brick slabs put above the fire to heat up to the cooking temperature. After that, the heated flat surface is removed, & food is placed on it to cook. As you can see, the traditional griddle-cooking process was demanding and left potential for various changes and growth. One of the most performing griddle is the Blackstone one. This firm wanted a cooking device that could fulfill the activities of a typical indoor cooking appliance while also being able to barbecue like a grill in the early 2000s. By 2005, they had developed their cornerstone product, the 36" Blackstone Griddle, which launched the company's lengthy line of griddle-cooking goods.

The Blackstone griddle is a basic and easy-to-use outdoor gas griddle made by the Blackstone Company. The griddle is made of professional-grade, high-quality stainless steel that is covered in a black powder coating to prevent rusting and extend the griddle's lifespan. The griddle's main feature is its 28-inch cooking surface, which is made of 7-gauge cold-rolled steel. It has the capacity to cook a huge number of dishes in a single batch.

The Blackstone gas griddle's best feature is that it comes with two different gas controller switches. This will aid in the creation of two distinct cooking zones on even a single cooking surface. It means that your food can be cooked at two different temperatures at the same time. Both burners are capable of producing 30000 BTU of heat when used simultaneously. The temperature settings range from high to low, allowing you to adapt according to your recipe's requirements. This guide covers everything there is to know about the Blackstone griddle or similar starting with the basics. What is the purpose of a griddle? The book discusses all of the advantages of a gas griddle, as well as some tips and tactics for becoming a master griddle cook.

Our goal is to teach you everything you need to know about the gas grill, including how it works, how to get the most out of it, and how to use it properly.

After providing you a broad overview, we'll show you loads of delectable recipes ranging from breakfast to fish, meat to vegan and vegetarian options.

Before we go into detail about how to use the Outdoor Gas Griddle, it's important to understand what it is. It's about a gas-powered grill that allows you to cook in a "restaurant-style" manner.

Whoever designed the Outdoor Grill had the vision of providing the best outdoor cooking experiences for large groups or families back in the day.

They've designed a griddle with a large flat-top grill that's ideal for breakfast, lunch, & dinner.

It's ideal for making eggs, pancakes, potatoes, quesadillas, grilled cheese, steaks, and other grilled dishes, among other things.

A lower shelf & two side shelves are also available for storing and preparing food.

This will be the best outdoor experience you've ever had. So let's begin.

Introduction to the Outdoor Gas Griddle

Outdoor gas Griddles are one of our favorite kitchen items because they can be used to cook nearly anything. You may use them to cook pancakes, fry bacon, and even bake a cake! They're composed of cast iron with a chrome finish, so they maintain heat evenly and are perfect for searing a steak. They are also very easy to store because they can be folded flat. In reality, it is the best product of its kind because it lacks the springs and hinges that cause other models to fail over time.

As anticipated before one of the best ones is the Blackstone griddle. They have won numerous honors, including Gourmet's 2009 Best Buy Award & Cooking Light Magazine's Taster's Choice Award in 2009. Roasting, searing, frying, and baking are all possibilities with this product. It's also collapsible, which makes it really easy to store. The fact that Blackstone griddles are composed of cast-iron material that has been seasoned with a specific blend of oils to prevent rusting is one of our favorite features. It's quite sturdy, making it ideal for use in a frying pan, inside a grill, or on the stovetop.

The Blackstone griddle is 21-1/2 inches long and features four baking surfaces that are 12 inches apart. These cast-iron countertop griddles are designed to keep heat in. They have an enamel surface that is easy to clean and won't rust or stain like traditional cast iron pans. When you're searing a steak, each surface has a textured finish knob that lets you manage the heat. The Blackstone griddle is long-lasting and well-made, and it has shown to be resistant to the elements throughout time. It's also quite simple to clean because you can simply wipe it down with a damp cloth or throw it in the dishwasher. The Blackstone griddle is available in two colors: black and red, making it ideal for any kitchen!

To summarize, a Blackstone griddle is an excellent tool for producing a variety of delectable dishes. It can be used to cook anything from eggs to pancakes to meat without moving around your cooktop, trying to get your pan to heat up evenly.

Benefits of Using an Outdoor Gas Griddle

An outdoor gas griddle is a wonderful method to feed a crowd while also keeping your breakfast or lunch location busy. If you consider the Blackstone griddle it has a revolutionary design that includes all of the characteristics of a traditional grill, plus an extra open area for pancakes, eggs, bacon, and more! Three stainless steel cooking surfaces are removable from this flat top grill. With just enough headroom to allow bread slices and buns, the heated bottom area is ideal for cooking classic foods like burgers or sausages.

The center component has two completely adjustable burners that may be set up in a "V" arrangement or parallel to accommodate various pan sizes currently available on the market. A gas-powered griddle with a cast aluminum top makes up the third part.

Health Benefits

Cooking over the an outdoor gas riddle has health benefits vs cooking into the stove or in the oven.

We'll go over a few of the health benefits. Let's look at the 4 key health advantages.

1. You are Consuming Less Fat

You eat less fat when you bbq because the drops of fat from the grates. Consider yourself the difference between cooking the burger on the griddle versus onto the stove. The renders of fat on the griddle. Because the fat onto the stovetop has no place to go, it pools and therefore is it is absorbed by the meat.

2. Griddled Vegetables Are Much Better for Your Health

Most of the people are unaware that when veggies are griddled, they retain more of the vitamins & minerals. This is particularly true of veggies with the low water content.

3. You are Using Less Butter

You'll have juicy cuts of the meat & delectable veggies if you master the griddling and don't overcook the food. You'll be less likely to actually reach for the butter or the other condiments to fancy up the dish because your griddle seals in much more moisture. Not only do you eat fewer calories, but you also eat fewer unhealthy substances.

4. Griddling Pairs Well with Outdoor Activities

Griddling is a good way to go outside. While grilling the dinner, many parents toss out a Frisbee or kick the ball across their yard with their kids. Cooking & dining outside stimulates the greater movement, that we all aware is a great health benefit to go along with the tasty meal.

How to Choose the Perfect Outdoor Gas Griddle

The key to enjoying an Outdoor Gas Griddle is to find the perfect flat-top to match your specific needs. This guide walks you through the different characteristics to consider.

Flat top size

Flat-top griddle sizes typically range among 17-inch, 22-inch, 28-inch, & 36-inch.

When selecting a size, consider the number of people you will be serving food to & if you want the griddle to be portable or not.

Gas or Electric

Even though we are mainly talking about the gas griddle you may want to consider an electric griddle. Electric griddle also have different cooking surface sizes and and are suitable for both indoor and outdoor use.

Electric flat-top griddles feature a non-stick simple flat-top griddle surface. However, gas flat-top griddles must be seasoned and cared for properly. Gas griddles give your meal a greater sear and flavor, but electric griddles are also much easier to clean afterward. Each series of griddles has its own set of advantages and disadvantages, so find out what works best for you & your family.

Combination Features

Combinations of a gas griddle and a grill are becoming increasingly common. All of the units have a griddle, which comes in a variety of sizes, and one of the following features: Air fryers, deep fryers, side burners, or grills are all options.

Accessories

There are typically numerous Accessories to choose from. Connected Hard Cover, Soft Cover, Cutting Board, Side Shelf, Garbage Bag Holder, With or Without Stand, Grease Management System Position, Locking Swivel Caster Wheels.

Basics on How to Use the Griddle

The Basics on Getting the Griddle Ready

After you've taken the Griddle out of the box, double-check that you have all of the supplied parts and fasteners by consulting the user manual.

The typical griddle's operation technique and working mechanism are identical to those of other classic griddles. The following general step-by-step instructions are applicable to many models and will show you how to use your griddle with ease.

Ensure the battery is properly inserted in the ignition switch before turning on your griddle.

Make that the propane gas cylinder is properly attached to the gas pipe. Switch on the gas and let it out through the gas control valve.

Start your griddle by turning the gas control valve to the High position and pressing the ignition switch until you hear a flame.

Always warm the griddle for 3 to 5 minutes before placing your meal on the frying surface for optimum results.

Now you can cook whatever you want on your griddle.

Pre-Startup Suggestions

Make sure the griddle plate is positioned properly in the four holes (2 on each side)

Wipe the cast iron griddle using a moist cloth till it is clean and debris-free, then dry fully.

Before you start cooking, make sure all gas connections are tight and that there are no leaks.

In the igniter button, place the battery. Remove the screw, insert the battery, and tighten the screw with your fingers.

Make sure all of the shelves (bottom and sides) are secure.

Make that the casters are in place and the locks are in working order.

Make sure your propane tank is brand new and has an OPD valve.

Place the griddle in a wind-protected area if at all possible.

First Startup Suggestions

Make sure the griddle plate is positioned properly in the four holes (2 on each side)

Make sure your propane tank is brand new and has an OPD valve. If you're unsure, ask one of our knowledgeable staff members.

Maintain a Propane tank that is at least half full or half empty.

Place the griddle in a wind-protected area if at all possible.

Turn on the propane stove.

Set the left burner to high (near the igniter button).

Do not look down into the space in between the griddle and the burners; instead, press the igniter button & listen for the ticking.

You should hear ticking followed by the first burner lighting up. Allow 30 seconds for the burner to heat up.

Restart the operation on the second burner.

Rep with ALL of the burners till the griddle is completely lighted.

Learning how to use the controls

Griddles are beneficial for a variety of reasons. They may use strongly concentrated heat to sear vegetables and meat while releasing the flavors of a well-cooked steak.

If you have the Blackstone Griddle it has a temperature control that allows you to fine-tune your cooking technique and maximize taste or texture. It comes with two replaceable cast iron plates that allow you to switch between searing & griddling on the go with no effort! And there's no need to scrub it afterward; simply deactivate the flame on the gas burner with one lever, then wipe down the counters before bedtime.

Legs on a Griddle

The foldable griddle legs on the Blackstone griddle make it easy to move your griddle around. These legs also include a caster wheel that allows you to correctly change the griddle position, as well as a lock mechanism to keep the griddle stable while cooking your food.

Switch for Gas Control

The gas controller switch is used to manage the gas flame and the temperature of the griddle cooking surface. It has a range of settings from high to low; you can adjust the settings to suit your preferences. Both gas controllers work independently, allowing you to cook a range of items while adjusting two distinct temperature settings at the same time.

Starting the grilling

You can make practically anything with an Outdorr Gas Griddle and get excellent results. In some models you can even cook different meals at different temperatures at the same time because they may have 4 independent zones. This allows you significantly more versatility.

Take the time to season the griddle before using it to keep your food from sticking. In the Pro Tips section, we'll go over the seasoning process. Once you've finished cooking, turn off the burners one by one, making careful to turn off the propane tank valve as well.

Pro Tips and FAQs

Pro tips

PRO
TIPS

Season the Surface of the Cooking

To ensure the best cooking results you must properly use seasoning. "What is seasoning?" you might wonder. There was only one way to keep food from sticking to the stove surface until non-stick coatings were invented. You will not only achieve a beautiful non-stick surface, but you will also protect the cooking surface from scratches & oxidation by generating a layer of burnt-on oil. Let's get this party started. To begin, thoroughly clean the cooking surface with a gentle or specific soap and water. To dry the surface, use a cloth. Apply a small amount of oil to the frying surface after that. Vegetable or canola oils with a high smoke point are the best to use. Spread the oil evenly across the frying surface with a paper towel. Set the temp at 275°F and turn on all four burners. Wait for the oil to start smoking and the surface to darken. Turn off the burners after the griddle has started to smoke and let it cool. Rep this step two or three times more until the entire area is equally black. Your griddle is now naturally non-stick and corrosion-resistant.

From Season to Season, Keep your Griddle in Use

Because you'll most likely keep your griddle outside, there are a few things you need to do before storing it and before using it again after it's been kept. Before storing, unplug the gas tank and store it away from the griddle with the valve closed. A griddle cover can also be purchased to keep insects and dust out. Make careful to examine the burner area for spider webs when you're ready to use your griddle again. If you don't wipe out the webs before cooking, they can catch fire and produce a flare-up. Check the level of gas in your tank to ensure that you have enough to begin cooking. It's a good idea to do a new season on the cooking surface once the tank is connected and you're ready to cook. Simply follow the steps above to restore your griddle to its former glory.

The Best Way to Clean a Griddle

You should clean your griddle after each usage, but it should not be washed like conventional pots and pans. You should avoid using dish soap to clean the cooking surface since you want to build up a great coating of seasoning to protect your griddle & get the best possible results. Most detergents contain a grease-cutting agent, which will eat straight through your seasoning coating. The best approach to clean your griddle is to use a griddle scraper & hot water like the pros do in restaurants. You can buy a griddle scraper to remove any remnants of food that have remained on the griddle without compromising the seasoning layer you've created. Most fats and sauces will dissolve in a wash with very hot water, which you may then scrape away with a knife. While you don't have to season your grill after each cleaning, doing so on a regular basis will keep your griddle dark and lustrous.

Invest in the Right Tools

To get the most out of your Griddle, you'll need professional-grade cooking gear. While you may have a variety of spatulas in your kitchen, we recommend investing in two long metal spatulas to get the most out of your griddle. These spatulas are not only long-lasting, but they also allow you to transport and turn a huge quantity of food at once. They're also thin and flexible, allowing you to scoop up full hash browns without spilling anything. At least one pair of long-handled metal tongs is also advised since they will allow you to reach everywhere on the griddle without getting burned.

Experiment with Various Cooking Fats

Unlike mabye standard grills, that allows cooking fat to fall into the coals or gas jets, the the best Griddles keep cooking fat where it belongs: on your food! As a result, you can play with different types of cooking fat to get the best results. Diverse oils not only impart different flavors, but they also act in different ways. Olive oil enriches meals by imparting a powerful and sometimes spicy black pepper flavor. The issue with olive oil is that it has a low smoke point, which means that once it reaches a certain temperature, it begins to taste burned. Use olive oil when cooking at a low to medium temperature, but avoid it when cooking at a high temperature. Try canola or ordinary vegetable oil if you're seeking for a high-heat cooking oil. They'll allow you to cook at high temperatures without getting a burnt taste. Butter, of course, has more taste than nearly everything else, but it also has a tendency to burn, so use it for low-heat cooking or quick-cooking meals.

The Perfect Burger

Mankind has been searching for the ideal burger for generations. Burger cooks have debated the best way to grind it, the best way to form the patties, and, of course, the best way to cook it since its inception. Some believe you need to utilize imported Japanese waygu meat, while others say the optimum method is high heat over charcoal. So, we're going to put an end to this dispute once and for all. The first step in making the finest burger you've ever had is to increase the fat content. When you go to the grocery, you usually have the option of choosing between 20 percent fat and 10% fat. This will not suffice for the perfect burger. The ideal burger contains between 25 and 30 percent fat, and the easiest way to achieve this is to grind it yourself with a mix of chuck and short rib meat. If you don't

want to do it yourself, inform your local butcher that you require ground beef with higher fat content. Also, make sure to use fresh ground beef whenever possible. Compacted beef is the enemy of the perfect burger, and the longer it sits in packaging, the more compressed it becomes.

Once you've found the appropriate beef, mold it into 1/3-pound loose balls. Don't overwork it, and don't squish the balls together; you want them to just hold together. Turn the burners to medium heat and light your griddle. You might believe that high heat is the greatest way to cook burgers, but this is not the case. Allow enough time for the fat to render and generate a delicious sear on your burgers. If you cook your burgers too quickly, they will be overdone and chewy on the inside. Place the ball on the griddle with a little vegetable oil drizzled over it. Press down with a grill weight to "smash" the burger as flat as possible. Do not mold it; simply push it onto the griddle and season with salt. To keep the burger flat, make an indentation in the center with your thumb. Flip, season with salt, and cook for the same amount of time after the first side has formed a good sear. Your burger will have more time to render fat and absorb it while it cooks this way. Remove it from the griddle, and then let it rest for five minutes once you've reached the desired temperature. Add whatever toppings you want and enjoy the finest burger you've ever tasted.

Maintenance Tips

To extend the life of your griddle, it must be properly stored and maintained. The tips below will show you how to maintain your griddle.

Clean your Griddle After Each Usage

When you first use your griddle, it will automatically season itself after each use. Cleaning is a crucial part of keeping your griddle clean & sanitary. Clean the griddle surface with hot water & a paper towel. To clean the cooking surface, do not use soapy water. Clean the cooking area with a scrapper. Clean and dry paper towels can be used to wipe down the greasy surface.

Get Rid of Rust

If you notice any rust spots on the griddle, scrape them thoroughly with 40 or 60 low grit sandpaper or steel wool.

After Cleaning, Coat the Griddle

After cleaning the griddle, apply a thin coat of cooking spray to the cooking surface to prevent rust from forming on the griddle's overcooking surface area.

Griddle Storage and Care

After you've completed all of the cleaning instructions, store your griddle somewhere cold and dry. Always keep your griddle covered & away from the humid region to avoid dust.

Frequently Asked Questions

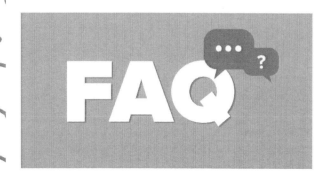

Below are some of the most often asked questions.

What Can You Make with A Griddle?

Griddles offer a wide range of cooking options. From traditional fare such as steak, burgers, and vegetables to more unusual fare such as stir-fry, pancakes, biscuits, & pizza (yes, pizza!).

Sure, a grill could smoke meat (sometimes), but that's about all it can do outside of your griddle. A griddle, on the other hand, can accomplish a lot more.

"A Griddle can do everything the grill could do and about 100 more things your grill can't," and I think that pretty much sums it up.

When Seasoning a Griddle, How Much Does It Take?

It's crucial to season a fresh Griddle! The performance of your griddle is determined by its seasoning and ability to cook on a non-stick, well-seasoned surface.

It takes around 30-45 minutes to season the griddle for the very first time. Take your time and get it perfect; despite your mind racing with the griddling delights, this isn't a process you want to rush through.

Is It Possible to Boil Water On a Griddle?

Another often asked question, griddles can boil a huge pot of water; however, due to a variety of variables, it takes nearly twice as long to bring a pot of water to the boil as it would on a regular burner.

Yes, you may boil water on a griddle; however, unless it's a last resort, We'd recommend boiling water the traditional way.

Is it True that a Griddle is Healthier than a Grill?

Another leading question, but one that is also fair. Here's the deal: It all boils down to two primary variables, which We'll go into in detail below:

A griddle can be healthier if you prepare nutritious food, to begin with, but at the end of each day, your cooking gear has the least impact on your overall health, what you give your body has the most impact on health.

But....

A griddle is often healthier than a grill since it allows you to enjoy outside cooking while grilling. However, a griddle does not emit the same carcinogens which a grill does because it is actively burning beneath your food and generating the char and pollutants that a traditional grill produces.

What Is the Distinction Between a Griddle and A Flat-Top Grill?

This is a very popular question, and it's reasonable because the two don't have an obvious differentiation.

A flat top griddle is essentially a griddle, and a griddle is essentially a flat top grill. We are not sure whenever these two terms started to be used interchangeably, but it's a widespread misunderstanding.

The term "flat top grill" refers to a grill with a flat top cooking surface instead of a grated grill, such as one found on a BBQ grill.

Is It Possible to Season a Griddle Using Butter?

If you ask around for suggestions for how to season your griddle, you'll get everything from a pound of bacon to a pat of butter. Seasoning using butter (or bacon) is, unfortunately, incorrect and lousy advice.

While bacon will contribute a lot of fat and grease to your new griddle surface, it won't give it a proper seasoning because most modern bacon has sugar, salt, as well as other additives that will sabotage the seasoning process & prevent the griddle surface from developing the true life-long connection you seek.

Despite popular belief, bacon should not be used as an initial seasoning.

Is it Necessary to Clean the Griddle After Each Use?

Yes, the griddle should be cleaned after each usage. It's critical to realize that cleaning the griddle isn't the same as washing your other pots and pans.

Soap or chemicals should not be used to clean the griddle.

When cleaning your griddle, first heat it up, scrape off any excess food, and then squirt water on the heated surface using the griddle bottles to generate a boiling/disinfecting action on the griddle surface.

Repeat this process till you are satisfied with the results, and then keep your griddle with a thin layer of oil on it to prevent corrosion and aid in long-term seasoning.

Conversion Tables of the Various Units of Measurement

CONVERSION CHART

Liquid Measure

8 ounces =	1 cup
2 cups =	1 pint
16 ounces =	1 pint
4 cups =	1 quart
1 gill =	1/2 cup or 1/4 pint
2 pints =	1 quart
4 quarts =	1 gallon
31.5 gal. =	1 barrel

3 tsp =	1 tbsp
2 tbsp =	1/8 cup or 1 fluid ounce
4 tbsp =	1/4 cup
8 tbsp =	1/2 cup
1 pinch =	1/8 tsp or less
1 tsp =	60 drops

Conversion of US Liquid Measure to Metric System

1 fluid oz. =	29.573 milliliters
1 cup =	230 milliliters
1 quart =	.94635 liters
1 gallon =	3.7854 liters
.033814 fluid ounce =	1 milliliter
3.3814 fluid ounces =	1 deciliter
33.814 fluid oz. or 1.0567 qt.=	1 liter

Dry Measure

2 pints =	1 quart
4 quarts =	1 gallon
8 quarts =	2 gallons or 1 peck
4 pecks =	8 gallons or 1 bushel
16 ounces =	1 pound
2000 lbs. =	1 ton

Conversion of US Weight and Mass Measure to Metric System

.0353 ounces =	1 gram
1/4 ounce =	7 grams
1 ounce =	28.35 grams
4 ounces =	113.4 grams
8 ounces =	226.8 grams
1 pound =	454 grams
2.2046 pounds =	1 kilogram
.98421 long ton or 1.1023 short tons =	1 metric ton

Linear Measure

12 inches =	1 foot
3 feet =	1 yard
5.5 yards =	1 rod
40 rods =	1 furlong
8 furlongs (5280 feet) =	1 mile
6080 feet =	1 nautical mile

Conversion of US Linear Measure to Metric System

1 inch =	2.54 centimeters
1 foot =	.3048 meters
1 yard =	.9144 meters
1 mile =	1609.3 meters or 1.6093 kilometers
.03937 in. =	1 millimeter
.3937 in.=	1 centimeter
3.937 in.=	1 decimeter
39.37 in.=	1 meter
3280.8 ft. or .62137 miles =	1 kilometer

To convert a Fahrenheit temperature to Centigrade, do the following:
a. Subtract 32   b. Multiply by 5   c. Divide by 9

To convert Centigrade to Fahrenheit, do the following:
a. Multiply by 9   b. Divide by 5   c. Add 32

Typical Griddle Temperature Chart

No.	Heat Levels	Temperature
1	Low	250 to 320°F
2	Medium	320 to 375°F
3	High	375 to 450°F or more

Breakfast Recipes

Kale Omelet

(Preparation time: 5 minutes | Cooking time: 10 minutes | Servings: 3)

Per serving: Calories 410, Total fat 27g, Protein 26g, Carbs 10g

Ingredients:

- 1 tablespoon of fresh sage, chopped
- 4 eggs
- 1/2 teaspoon of pepper
- 4 cups of kale, chopped
- 1/2 teaspoon of salt
- 1/3 cup of parmesan cheese, grated

Instructions:

- Preheat your griddle to medium-high temperature.
- Coat the top of the griddle using cooking spray.
- Cook for a few minutes, or till kale has wilted, on a heated griddle top.
- In a mixing bowl, whisk together the eggs, then add the parmesan, sage, pepper, & salt. Pour the egg mixture over kale.
- Cook for around 8-10 minutes, or till the egg mixture is stiff.
- Enjoy your servings.

Breakfast Sandwich with Bacon and Swiss Cheese

(Preparation time: 10 minutes | Cooking time: 15 minutes | Servings: 2)

Per serving: Calories 470, Total fat 21g, Protein 38g, Carbs 10g

Ingredients:

- 4 tablespoons of Swiss grated cheese
- 4 round rolls sandwiches
- 4 tablespoons of ketchup
- 2 slices of bacon
- Salt and pepper to taste

Instructions:

- Begin by removing the tops of the sandwiches.
- Remove the inside section of the sandwiches with a spoon, being careful not to damage or crack the crust.
- Fill each sandwich using a small amount of ketchup.
- Place the bacon on top of the tomato, cut it into little pieces.
- Preheat your Blackstone Griddle at 400°F for direct cooking in the meanwhile.
- Brush an oven-safe baking pan using olive oil.
- Arrange the sandwiches inside the pan, spacing them out as much as possible.
- Finish with a sprinkling of salt and pepper, followed by the grated Swiss cheese.
- Put the pan onto the griddle and cook for around 15 minutes.
- Remove as soon as it's done and serve right away.

Spinach and Egg Scramble

(Preparation time: 5 minutes | Cooking time: 10 minutes | Servings: 1)

Per serving: Calories 335, Total fat 27g, Protein 19g, Carbs 6g

Ingredients:

- 1/2 cup of spinach, chopped

- 3 eggs, lightly beaten
- Salt and pepper to taste
- 4 mushrooms, chopped
- 1/4 cup of bell peppers, chopped

Instructions:

- Preheat the griddle at medium-high temperature.
- Coat the top of the griddle using cooking spray.
- Place chopped vegetables on top of a hot griddle and cook till softened.
- Stir in the eggs, pepper, & salt till the eggs are scrambled and set.
- Enjoy your servings.

Cheese and Olive Omelet

(Preparation time: 5 minutes | Cooking time: 10 minutes | Servings: 4)

Per serving: Calories 252, Total fat 23g, Protein 10g, Carbs 1g

Ingredients:

- 2 tablespoons of olive oil
- 8 olives, pitted
- 4 large eggs
- 1 teaspoon of herb de Provence
- 1/2 teaspoon of salt
- 4 tablespoons of cheese

Instructions:

- In a mixing dish, whisk together the eggs, olives, herb de Provence, salt, & olive oil.
- Preheat your griddle at medium-high temperature.
- Coat the top of the griddle using cooking spray.
- Cook for around 3 minutes on a heated griddle top or till the omelet is softly golden brown.
- Cook for another 2 minutes after flipping the omelet.
- Serve and have fun.

French Toast Sticks

(Preparation time: 10 minutes | Cooking time: 10 minutes | Servings: 2)

Per serving: Calories 166, Total fat 7g, Protein 10g, Carbs 14g

Ingredients:

- 2/3 cup of milk
- 2 eggs
- 1 teaspoon of vanilla
- 4 bread slices, cut each bread slice into 3 pieces vertically
- 1/4 teaspoon of ground cinnamon

Instructions:

- Preheat your griddle to a low temperature.
- Whisk together the eggs, cinnamon, vanilla, & milk in a mixing dish.
- Coat the top of the griddle using cooking spray.
- Dip each slice of bread into the egg mixture & coat thoroughly.
- Place the coated bread pieces on the hot griddle top & cook till both sides are golden brown.
- Enjoy your meal.

Simple Cheese Sandwich

(Preparation time: 10 minutes | Cooking time: 10 minutes | Servings: 1)

Per serving: Calories 340, Total fat 26g, Protein 15g, Carbs 10g

Ingredients:

- 2 teaspoons of butter
- 2 bread slices
- 2 cheese slices

Instructions:

- Preheat your griddle to a low temperature.
- Arrange cheese slices on top of one slice of bread and cover with another slice of bread.
- Both bread pieces should be slathered in butter.
- Cook the sandwich on a hot griddle till golden brown and the cheese has melted.
- Enjoy your meal.

Tomato Scrambled Egg

(Preparation time: 5 minutes | Cooking time: 10 minutes | Servings: 2)

Per serving: Calories 125, Total fat 12g, Protein 6g, Carbs 1g

Ingredients:

- 1 tablespoon of olive oil
- 2 eggs, lightly beaten
- Salt and pepper to taste
- 2 tablespoons of fresh basil, chopped
- 1/2 tomato, chopped

Instructions:

- Preheat your griddle at medium-high temperature.
- Apply oil to the griddle's surface.
- Cook till the tomatoes have softened.
- Combine together the eggs, basil, pepper, & salt.
- Cook till the eggs are set on top of the tomatoes by pouring the egg mixture over them.
- Enjoy your meal.

Watermelon Honey Breakfast Salad with Icecream

(Preparation time: 10 minutes | Cooking time: 5 minutes | Servings: 4)

Per serving: Calories 180, Total fat 6g, Protein 4g, Carbs 16g

Ingredients:

- 4 tablespoons of brown sugar
- 2 cups of vanilla ice cream
- 4 slices of watermelon of 7 oz. each
- 1 lime
- 2 tablespoons of honey
- 10 mint leaves

Instructions:

- Preheat the Blackstone griddle for around 10 minutes at 370°F (direct cooking) with the lid closed.

- Prepare the mint syrup in the meantime.
- Mint leaves should be washed and dried before being finely chopped.
- In a mixing bowl, combine the mint leaves and sugar.
- Stir in the sugar & mint till they're completely combined.
- Watermelon slices should be washed and dried.
- Squeeze the lime juice into a dish and drain it.
- Mix in the honey till you have a nice, uniform emulsion.
- Place the watermelon slices on the grill after brushing them with the emulsion.
- Cook for around 1 minute on each side of the watermelon slices.
- Place the watermelon on serving plates after removing it from the grill.
- Mint sugar should be sprinkled on the watermelon slices.
- Serve the vanilla ice cream on top of the dishes.

Ricotta Cheese and Pistachio Sandwich

(Preparation time: 5 minutes | Cooking time: 15 minutes | Servings: 4)

Per serving: Calories 250, Total fat 10g, Protein 19g, Carbs 18g

Ingredients:

- 8 slices of whole meal bread
- 6 tablespoons of melted butter
- 1/2 cup of ricotta cheese
- 4 tablespoons of pistachio cream

Instructions:

- Preheat the Blackstone griddle at 410°F for high-temperature grilling and direct cooking.
- Brush each side of the bread slices using butter.
- Spread pistachio cream in the center of four slices
- Brush 2 slices of bread with ricotta cheese and top with the remaining slices to create 4 sandwiches.
- Into the Blackstone griddle, place the sandwiches.

- Cook for around 10-12 minutes, watching to see if the cheese has entirely melted.
- Cut and serve while still warm.

Porcini Mushrooms Garlic and Bacon Omelet

(Preparation time: 10 minutes | Cooking time: 30 minutes | Servings: 4)

Per serving: Calories 292, Total fat 14g, Protein 23g, Carbs 2g

Ingredients:

- 1 garlic clove
- 1 1/4 cups of porcini mushrooms, cleaned
- 1/2 cup of sliced bacon
- 5 eggs
- 4 teaspoons of olive oil
- 1 tablespoon of chives
- 1 pinch of salt

Instructions:

- Begin by cleaning and cutting the chives.
- Garlic cloves should also be peeled and washed.
- Clean the porcini mushrooms before slicing them into 1/4-inch thin pieces.
- Thinly slice the bacon slices.
- Sauté whole garlic clove & mushrooms in olive oil in a sauté pan over medium flame till soft.
- Add the bacon and cook for 1 minute after they are cooked.
- Remove the clove of garlic.
- Remove the mushrooms from the flame and set them to cool on a dry kitchen towel.
- Preheat a zone of the Blackstone griddle at 370°F in the meantime (direct cooking).
- Crack 3 eggs into a mixing dish with the chives & whisk thoroughly and forcefully with a teaspoon of salt.
- In a baking pan, put the eggs, then add the garlic, bacon, & porcini combination.
- Place the baking pan on the Blackstone griddle and cook for around 15 minutes with the lid closed.
- Stick a knife into the center of your omelet to check for doneness; if the knife comes out clean, your omelet is ready to eat.

Pineapple Breakfast Salad with Maple Syrup Sauce

(Preparation time: 10 minutes | Cooking time: 15 minutes | Servings: 4)

Per serving: Calories 90, Total fat 1g, Protein 1g, Carbs 14g

Ingredients:

- 1 cup of maple syrup
- 1 teaspoon of ground cinnamon
- 1 whole pineapple
- 2 tablespoons of sugar
- 1 teaspoon of vanilla essence
- 1 lemon

Instructions:

- Prepare one zone of the Blackstone grill for the direct cooking by preheating it at 390°F for 10 minutes.
- The pineapple should be peeled, washed, and dried before being divided into four sections.
- Place the pineapple straight on the griddle after sprinkling it with sugar.
- Cook for around 15 minutes with the lid closed, turning the pineapple occasionally.
- Make the maple syrup sauce in the meantime.
- In a saucepan, combine the syrup and the water.
- Mix in the vanilla and cinnamon.
- Turn off the flame and leave aside for around 5 minutes, stirring regularly.
- Remove the pineapple from the griddle as soon as it is done cooking and set it on serving plates.
- Serve with a dollop of maple syrup sauce on top of the pineapple.

Peanut Butter and Vanilla Toast

(Preparation time: 10 minutes | Cooking time: 10 minutes | Servings: 3)

Per serving: Calories 390, Total fat 14g, Protein 11g, Carbs 29g

Ingredients:

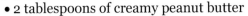

- 2 tablespoons of creamy peanut butter
- 1 cup of brown sugar
- 1 loaf of toast bread
- 1 teaspoon of grape jelly
- 1 tablespoon butter
- 1 teaspoon of vanilla extract
- ¾ cup of half and half

Instructions:

- Make a typical PB&J sandwich with the desired jelly-to-peanut-butter ratio.
- Combine two eggs, 1 teaspoon of vanilla, 1 cup of brown sugar, and 3/4 cup of half & half in a medium-sized mixing dish.
- Melt 1 tablespoon of butter on the griddle (medium-high temperature, 350°F, direct cooking).
- Cook for around 3-5 minutes on the griddle after dipping and coating the PB&J in the mixture.
- Cook for another 3-5 minutes on the other side.
- Serve while it's still hot.

Caprese Omelet

(Preparation time: 10 minutes | Cooking time: 10 minutes | Servings: 2)

Per serving: Calories 515, Total fat 40g, Protein 37g, Carbs 5g

Ingredients:

- 1 tablespoon of fresh basil
- 6 eggs
- Salt and pepper to taste
- 1/2 cup of cherry tomatoes, cut in halves
- 1/2 cup of mozzarella cheese, sliced

Instructions:

- Preheat your griddle at a low setting.
- In a mixing dish, whisk together the eggs, pepper, & salt. Add the basil and mix well.
- Coat the top of the griddle using cooking spray.
- Sauté tomatoes for a few minutes on a heated griddle top.
- Pour the egg mixture over the tomatoes and let it sit for a few minutes till the eggs are somewhat hard.

- Allow the omelet to set before adding the mozzarella cheese slices.
- Enjoy your meal.

Spicy Egg Crumbled

(Preparation time: 10 minutes | Cooking time: 10 minutes | Servings: 2)

Per serving: Calories 355, Total fat 33g, Protein 12g, Carbs 3g

Ingredients:

- 1 tomato, diced
- 4 eggs
- 1 Serrano chili pepper, chopped
- 1/4 teaspoon of pepper
- 2 tablespoons of cilantro, chopped
- 1/2 teaspoon of salt
- 1/3 cup of heavy cream
- 3 tablespoons of butter
- 2 tablespoons of scallions, sliced

Instructions:

- Preheat your griddle at medium-high temperature.
- Over the top of the hot griddle, melt the butter.
- Sauté for around 2 minutes with the tomato and chili pepper.
- Whisk together eggs, cilantro, cream, pepper, & salt in a mixing dish.
- Stir the egg mixture into the tomato and chili pepper till the egg is set.
- Serve with scallions as a garnish.

Broccoli Omelet

(Preparation time: 10 minutes | Cooking time: 10 minutes | Servings: 2)

Per serving: Calories 203, Total fat 16g, Protein 12g, Carbs 4g

Ingredients:

- 1 tablespoon of olive oil
- 4 eggs
- 1/2 teaspoon of salt
- 1 cup of broccoli, chopped and cooked
- 1/4 teaspoon of pepper

Instructions:

- In a mixing dish, whisk together eggs, pepper, & salt.
- Preheat your griddle to medium-high temperature. Oil the griddle's surface.
- Cook till the broccoli & egg mixture is set on the hot griddle top. Cook till the omelet is softly golden brown on the other side.
- Enjoy your meal.

Classic Denver Omelet

(Preparation time: 10 minutes | Cooking time: 10 minutes | Servings: 2)

Per serving: Calories 507, Total fat 40g, Protein 31g, Carbs 5g

Ingredients:

- 1/4 cup of green bell pepper, chopped
- 6 large eggs
- Salt and black pepper
- 1/4 cup of country ham, diced
- 1/4 teaspoon of cayenne pepper
- 1/4 cup of yellow onion, finely chopped
- 2/3 cup of cheddar cheese, shredded
- 2 tablespoons of butter

Instructions:

- Preheat the griddle to medium temperature and spread the butter on it.
- Cook the ham, onion, & pepper in the butter till the veggies have softened somewhat.
- In a large-sized mixing dish, whisk together the eggs with a pinch of salt & cayenne pepper.
- On the griddle, divide the vegetables into two parts and top each with half of the eggs. Cook till the eggs have started to firm up, then top each omelet with cheese.
- Remove the omelet from the griddle by folding them over. Serves right away.

Gruyere and Bacon Omelet

(Preparation time: 10 minutes | Cooking time: 15 minutes | Servings: 2)

Per serving: Calories 434, Total fat 55g, Protein 55g, Carbs 3g

Ingredients:

- 1/4 lb. of gruyere, shredded

- 6 eggs, beaten
- 1 tablespoon of chives, finely chopped
- 6 strips of bacon
- 1 teaspoon of black pepper
- Vegetable oil
- 1 teaspoon of salt

Instructions:

- Set aside for 10 minutes after adding salt to the beaten eggs.
- Place the bacon strips onto the griddle over medium temperature. Cook till the bacon is still pliable, and most of the fat has been rendered. Place the bacon on paper towels after removing it from the griddle.
- Chop the bacon into small pieces once it has been drained.
- Pour the eggs into two uniform pools on the griddle. Cook till the eggs' bottoms begin to firm up. Cook the eggs with the gruyere till the cheese has melted & the eggs are just beginning to color.
- Add the bacon slices and fold one half of the omelet over the other using a spatula. Remove them from the griddle, season using pepper and chives, and serve.

Sausage and Veggie Scramble

(Preparation time: 10 minutes | Cooking time: 20 minutes | Servings: 4)

Per serving: Calories 342, Total fat 25g, Protein 23g, Carbs 6g

Ingredients:

- 1 green bell pepper, sliced
- 8 eggs, beaten
- 1 teaspoon of salt
- 1/2 lb. of sausage, sliced into thin rounds or chopped
- 1 yellow onion, sliced
- Vegetable oil
- 1 cup of white mushrooms, sliced
- 1/2 teaspoon of black pepper

Instructions:

- Preheat your griddle to a medium-high temperature.
- Add the peppers & mushrooms to the griddle after brushing it with vegetable oil. After a few minutes, add the onions and cook till they are lightly browned. Cook till the onions are tender, seasoning using salt and pepper.
- Mix the sausage with the vegetables on the griddle. Cook till they are gently browned.
- Cook till the eggs are done to your liking, then add the eggs & mix them in with the vegetables. Remove the scramble out from the griddle with a big spatula and serve immediately.

Nutella and Almond Toast

(Preparation time: 10 minutes | Cooking time: 15 minutes | Servings: 3)

Per serving: Calories 420, Total fat 20g, Protein 5g, Carbs 35g

-

Ingredients:

- 2 tablespoons of Nutella cream
- 1 cup of brown sugar
- 1 tablespoon of butter
- 1 loaf of whole meal Toast bread
- ¾ cup of half and half
- 1 teaspoon of almond milk
- 1 teaspoon of vanilla extract

Instructions:

- To begin, whisk together two eggs, 1 teaspoon of vanilla, almond milk, 1 cup of brown sugar, and 3/4 cup of half & half in a medium-sized mixing dish.
- Melt one tablespoon of butter onto the griddle (medium-high temperature, at 350°F, direct cooking).
- Dip & coat the Nutella in the mixture before placing it on the griddle with the toast and cooking for around 3-5 minutes.
- Cook for another around 3-5 minutes on the other side.
- Serve while it's still hot.

French Toast Stuffed with Apple and Bourbon Caramel Sauce

(Preparation time: 10 minutes | Cooking time: 20 minutes | Servings: 4)

Per serving: Calories 322, Total fat 17g, Protein 12g, Carbs 32g

Ingredients:

- 2/3 cup of white sugar
- 1 cup of softened cream cheese
- 8 thick slices of French bread
- ¼ cup of whole milk
- 2 large green apples, small dice
- 3 cups of bourbon
- 2 tablespoons of cinnamon sugar
- ½ green apple brunoise (finely diced)

Egg mix:

- 4 eggs
- ¼ cup of milk
- 1 tablespoon of cinnamon sugar

Instructions:

- Add the apples, bourbon, & sugar to a large-sized sauté pan on medium-high flame. Bring to the boil, then reduce till the consistency is similar to maple syrup. Remove from the flame.
- Combine the cream cheese, finely diced apples, cinnamon sugar, and milk in a large-sized mixing bowl. Mix well to ensure that everything is uniformly distributed.
- Add the egg mixture components to a casserole dish and stir to combine evenly.
- Make sandwiches with a second piece of bread along with some of the cream cheese mixture on one side. Rep with the rest of the bread.
- Coat both sides of the sandwiches in the egg mixture. Cook the French toast sandwiches onto a griddle with a little oil or non-stick spray over medium flame. Cook each side for around 3-4 minutes.
- When the French toast is done, cut it in half and place it on a serving plate. Drizzle some of the cooked apples on top of the caramel sauce. Serve garnished with fresh mint or the powdered sugar.

Ham and Cheddar Sandwiches

(Preparation time: 10 minutes | Cooking time: 15 minutes | Servings: 2)

Per serving: Calories 450, Total fat 18g, Protein 38g, Carbs 10g

Ingredients:

- 4 tablespoons of cheddar grated cheese
- 4 round rolls sandwiches
- Salt and pepper to taste
- 2 slices of raw ham
- 4 tablespoons of peeled tomatoes

Instructions:

- Begin by removing the tops of the sandwiches.
- Remove the inside section of the sandwiches with a spoon, being careful not to damage or split the crust.
- Fill each sandwich with a small amount of peeled tomato.
- Place the uncooked ham on top of the tomato, cut it into small pieces.
- Preheat the Blackstone griddle to high (430°F and direct cooking) in the meantime.
- Brush an oven-safe baking pan using olive oil.
- Arrange the sandwiches in the pan, spacing them out as much as possible.
- Season using salt and pepper, and then top with shredded cheddar cheese.
- Place the pan on the griddle for around 15 minutes to cook.
- Remove from the griddle as soon as it's done and serve right away.

Toad in a Hole

(Preparation time: 10 minutes | Cooking time: 10 minutes | Servings: 4)

Per serving: Calories 206, Total fat 11g, Protein 9g, Carbs 18g

Ingredients:

- 2 tablespoons of butter
- 4 slices white, wheat, or sourdough bread

- Salt and black pepper
- 4 eggs

Instructions:

- Preheat the griddle to medium temperature and distribute the butter evenly.
- Each piece of bread should have a hole in the center.
- Place the bread slices on the griddle & crack an egg into each hole in the bread.
- Cook till the bread is golden brown, then turn and continue cooking till the egg whites are hard.

Before serving, remove them from the griddle and season using salt and black pepper.

Mexican-Style Scramble

(Preparation time: 10 minutes | Cooking time: 10 minutes | Servings: 4)

Per serving: Calories 443, Total fat 54g, Protein 51g, Carbs 35g

Ingredients:

- 1/2 yellow onion
- 8 eggs, beaten
- 1/2 cup of jack cheese
- 1/2 teaspoon of black pepper
- 1 lb. of Chorizo
- 1 cup of cooked black beans
- Vegetable oil
- 1/2 cup of green chilies
- 1/4 cup of green onion, chopped

Instructions:

- Preheat the griddle at medium-high temperature. Place the Chorizo on one side and the onions on the other side of the griddle with oil.
- Combine the onion, Chorizo, beans, & chilies once the onion has softened.
- Add and cook till the eggs have reached the proper firmness, then add the cheese and green onion.
- Before serving, remove the scramble out from the griddle & season using black pepper.

Hash-Brown Scramble

(Preparation time: 10 minutes | Cooking time: 10 minutes | Servings: 4)

Per serving: Calories 470, Total fat 30g, Protein 31g, Carbs 19g

Ingredients:

- 1 cup of cheddar cheese
- 2 russet potatoes, shredded, rinsed and drained
- 1/3 cup of green onion, chopped
- 8 eggs, beaten
- 6 slices of bacon, cut into small pieces
- Vegetable oil

Instructions:

- Brush the griddle using vegetable oil and preheat it to medium.
- Place the potatoes on one side of the griddle and spread them out in a 1/2-inch-thick layer. Cook till golden brown on one side, then flip. Cook the bacon till the fat has rendered on the other side of the griddle.
- Stir in the bacon and green onion after adding the eggs & cheese to the top of the hash browns. Cook till the cheese has melted, then divide among four dishes evenly.

Classic French Toast

(Preparation time: 10 minutes | Cooking time: 10 minutes | Servings: 4)

Per serving: Calories 332, Total fat 11g, Protein 16g, Carbs 34g

Ingredients:

- 2 tablespoons of sugar
- 6 eggs, beaten
- Powdered sugar
- 1/4 cup of "half and half" or heavy cream
- 1 teaspoon of salt
- 8 slices of thick-cut white or sourdough bread
- 1 tablespoon of cinnamon
- Butter
- Maple syrup

Instructions:

- Preheat the griddle at medium.
- Combine the eggs, cream, sugar, cinnamon, and salt in a large mixing dish. Blend till smooth.
- Using butter or vegetable oil, lightly coat the griddle.
- Place each slice of bread on the griddle after thoroughly dipping it in the egg mixture.
- When the French toast has started to brown on one side, flip it and cook until the other side has also browned. Approximately four minutes.
- Remove the French toast from the griddle and serve with warm maple syrup and powdered sugar.

Burgers Recipe

Mini Onion Burgers

(Preparation time: 10 minutes | Cooking time: 15 minutes | Servings: 8)

Per serving: Calories 315, Total fat 23g, Protein 21g, Carbs 4g

Ingredients:

- 12 to 15 small potato rolls, split
- 1 red onion, sliced
- 1/2 to 1 teaspoon of cayenne pepper
- 1/4 teaspoon of salt
- 2 tablespoons of Dijon mustard
- 1 lb. of lean ground beef
- 1/8 teaspoon of pepper
- 6 tablespoons of mayonnaise
- Optional: mustard, catsup or mayonnaise

Instructions:

- Preheat the griddle at medium-high and brush a thin layer of the olive oil on it.
- Cook, occasionally stirring, till the onion is soft, around 10 minutes on the griddle; transfer to a bowl. Combine the meat, salt, & pepper in a separate bowl. Make small patties, approximately 2 inches in diameter. Cook patties for around 3 to 4 minutes on each side in a grill pan. In a small-sized bowl, combine

mayonnaise, mustard, and cayenne pepper for the Special Sauce. If preferred, top patties with grilled onion, Special Sauce, and other toppings on buns.

Korean Bulgogi Burgers

(Preparation time: 10 minutes | Cooking time: 15 minutes | Servings: 4)

Per serving: Calories 275, Total fat 16g, Protein 22g, Carbs 7g

Ingredients:

- ¾ cup of grated onion
- 3 tablespoons of soy sauce
- 1 tablespoon plus 2 teaspoons of dry sherry
- 1 pound of ground beef sirloin
- 1½ teaspoons of toasted sesame oil
- 1 tablespoon plus 1 teaspoon of sugar
- ½ teaspoon of coarsely ground black pepper
- 2 cloves of garlic, minced

Instructions:

- Gently combine the beef, 1/2 cup of onion, 1 teaspoon of sesame oil, 1 teaspoon of sugar, 1 tablespoon of soy sauce, the pepper, 1 tablespoon of sherry, & half of the garlic in a medium-sized mixing bowl. Form into four 3/4-inch thick patties.
- Combine the remaining 1/4 cup of onion, 1 tablespoon of sugar, 2 tablespoons of soy sauce, 1/2 teaspoon of sesame oil, 2 teaspoons of sherry, & garlic in a small-sized mixing bowl. Set aside for the final touch.
- Preheat the griddle at medium-high and brush a thin layer of the olive oil on it.
- Cook the burgers on the heated griddle till done to your liking, 3 to 5 minutes on each side for medium-rare.
- Serve it on a buttered, toasted hamburger or hoagie buns.
- Add the onion-soy sauce mixture & slivered scallions to finish (white and green parts).

Barbecue Cheese Burgers

(Preparation time: 10 minutes | Cooking time: 15 minutes | Servings: 6)

Per serving: Calories 236, Total fat 15g, Protein 19g, Carbs 15g

Ingredients:

- 2 cloves of garlic, minced
- ½ teaspoon of curry powder
- 1 cup of grated Monterey Jack or extra-sharp cheddar cheese
- 3 pounds of ground beef sirloin
- ½ teaspoon of coarsely ground black pepper
- ½ cup of mesquite-flavored barbecue sauce
- ½ small red onion halved and thinly sliced
- 1 tablespoon of chili powder
- ½ teaspoon of salt

Instructions:

- In a large-sized mixing dish, combine all of the ingredients except for the cheese and onion till well incorporated. Make 6 patties, each about 1 inch thick.
- Preheat the Blackstone griddle at medium-high and brush a thin layer of the olive oil on it.
- Cook the burgers on the heated griddle till done to your liking, about 5 minutes on each side, for the last minute of cooking, top with cheese and onion.
- Serve it with the toasted sesame seed burger buns or onion rolls.
- Finish it off with lettuce & tomato slices.

Best-Ever Cheddar Burgers

(Preparation time: 10 minutes | Cooking time: 20 minutes | Servings: 4)

Per serving: Calories 534, Total fat 29g, Protein 36g, Carbs 29g

Ingredients:

- 1/3 cup of fresh parsley, chopped
- 1 to 1-1/2 lbs. of ground turkey

- 1/4 cup of whole-berry cranberry sauce
- 4 buns, split and toasted
- 4 green onions, finely chopped
- 1 teaspoon of poultry seasoning
- 1 tablespoon of grill seasoning
- 1 Granny Smith apple, cored and thinly sliced
- 8 leaves of green leaf lettuce
- 2 tablespoons of oil
- 8 slices of Cheddar cheese
- 2 tablespoons of spicy brown mustard

Instructions:

- Preheat the Blackstone griddle at medium-high temperature and brush a thin layer of the olive oil on it.
- Form 4 patties from the turkey, parsley, onions, and seasonings. In a heated griddle. Place patties on the heated griddle and cook the patties for around 5 minutes on each side, or till no longer pink in the center. 2 to 3 apple slices & 2 cheese slices should be placed on top of each patty. Remove the patties and cover to allow the cheese to melt. Combine the cranberry sauce & mustard and spread it on the cut sides of the buns. Close sandwiches by adding lettuce and burgers.

Irene's Portabella Burgers

(Preparation time: 10 minutes | Cooking time: 20 minutes | Servings: 4)

Per serving: Calories 375, Total fat 22g, Protein 7g, Carbs 37g

Ingredients:

- 1 cup of Italian salad dressing
- 4 slices of Muenster or Gruyère cheese
- 4 portabella mushroom caps
- 4 sourdough buns, split
- For garnish: romaine lettuce

Instructions:

- Preheat the Blackstone griddle at medium-high temperature and brush a thin layer of the olive oil on it.
- In a plastic zip-top bag, combine the mushrooms and salad dressing, twisting to coat. Chill for 30 minutes, rotating once or twice. Remove the mushrooms and toss out the dressing. Grill mushrooms for 2 to 3 minutes on each side on the heated griddle. Grill buns for one minute, cut-side down, or till toasted. Serve the mushroom, cheese, and lettuce on top of the buns right away.

Gobblin' Good Turkey Burgers

(Preparation time: 10 minutes | Cooking time: 20 minutes | Servings: 4 to 6)

Per serving: Calories 668, Total fat 38g, Protein 49g, Carbs 28g

Ingredients:

- 1 onion, minced
- 1/2 teaspoon of dry mustard
- 1 lb. of ground turkey
- 4 to 6 hamburger buns, split
- 1 cup of shredded Cheddar cheese
- Salt and pepper to taste
- 1/4 cup of Worcestershire sauce

Instructions:

- Preheat the Blackstone griddle at medium-high temperature and brush a thin layer of the olive oil on it.
- Combine all ingredients except for the buns in a mixing bowl and shape into 4 to 6 patties. Cook on the griddle for around 4 to 5 minutes on each side till the desired doneness is achieved, then serve on the hamburger buns.

Italian Hamburgers

(Preparation time: 10 minutes | Cooking time: 20 minutes | Servings: 6)

Per serving: Calories 684, Total fat 28g, Protein 41g, Carbs 65g

Ingredients:

- 1 1/2 lbs. of ground beef
- 1/2 cup of Italian-flavored dry bread crumbs
- 6 hamburger buns, split
- 2 eggs, beaten
- 2 slices of bacon, crisply cooked and crumbled
- 0.7-oz. pkg. of Italian salad dressing mix
- 1 cup of shredded mozzarella cheese

Instructions:

- Combine all ingredients (excluding buns) in a large-sized mixing dish. Mix thoroughly and divide into 6 patties.
- Preheat the Blackstone griddle at medium-high temperature and brush a thin layer of the olive oil on it.
- Cook on the griddle till the desired level of doneness is reached for around 5 to 8 minutes on each side. On buns, serve.

Crunchy Chicken Burgers

(Preparation time: 10 minutes | Cooking time: 20 minutes | Servings: 4 to 6)

Per serving: Calories 566, Total fat 28g, Protein 41g, Carbs 38g

Ingredients:

- 1/4 cup of honey barbecue sauce
- 1/8 teaspoon of salt
- 1 lb. of ground chicken
- 3/4 cup of mini shredded wheat cereal, crushed
- 4 to 6 hamburger buns, split
- 1 egg, beaten
- 1/8 teaspoon of pepper

Instructions:

- Combine all ingredients, except for the buns, and shape into 4 to 6 patties.
- Preheat the Blackstone griddle at medium-high temperature and brush a thin layer of the olive oil on it.
- Cook for around 5 to 6 minutes per side, or till the center is no longer pink. On buns, serve alongside your favorite sauces and toppings.

Garlic & Mustard Burgers

(Preparation time: 10 minutes | Cooking time: 20 minutes | Servings: 4)

Per serving: Calories 576, Total fat 48g, Protein 31g, Carbs 25g

Ingredients:

- 5 garlic cloves, chopped
- 4 Monterey Jack cheese slices
- 1 lb. of ground beef
- 3 tablespoons of country-style Dijon mustard
- 4 hamburger buns, split
- 7-oz. jar of roasted red peppers, drained

Instructions:

- Preheat the Blackstone griddle at medium-high temperature and brush a thin layer of the olive oil on it.
- Combine the beef, mustard, & garlic in a mixing bowl. Form into four 3/4-inch thick patties. Place the patties on the heated griddle and cook patties for a total of around 6 to 10 minutes, depending on the desired doneness. Cheese and peppers go on top of burgers.

Bean & Chile Burgers

(Preparation time: 10 minutes | Cooking time: 20 minutes | Servings: 4)

Per serving: Calories 433, Total fat 27g, Protein 13g, Carbs 36g

-

Ingredients:

- 4-oz. can of green chilies
- 1/2 cup of cornmeal
- 1/4 teaspoon of garlic powder
- 16-oz. can of black beans, drained and rinsed
- 11-oz. can of corn, drained
- 4 sandwich buns, split
- 1 cup of cooked rice
- 1 teaspoon of onion powder
- salt to taste

- Optional: salsa

Instructions:

- Preheat the Blackstone griddle at medium-high temperature and brush a thin layer of the olive oil on it.
- In a large-sized mixing bowl, mash the beans, then add the corn, onion powder, chilies, rice, cornmeal, and garlic powder. Form the mixture into four big patties and season using salt. Add the patties on the griddle and cook till golden brown on both sides, around 4 to 5 minutes on each side. Serve on buns with salsa on the side, if desired.

Beverly's Bacon Burgers

(Preparation time: 10 minutes | Cooking time: 20 minutes | Servings: 7)

Per serving: Calories 397, Total fat 15g, Protein 33g, Carbs 31g

Ingredients:

- 2 carrots, peeled and grated
- 1-1/2 teaspoons of garlic, minced
- 1 1/2 lbs. of ground beef
- 7 slices of bacon
- 2 potatoes, peeled and chopped
- 1 teaspoon of salt
- 1 onion, grated
- 7 sandwich buns, split
- 2 eggs, beaten
- 1 to 2 teaspoons of dried parsley
- pepper to taste

Instructions:

- Combine all ingredients except for the bacon & buns in a mixing bowl and shape into 14 patties. Wrap each burger in a bacon slice & secure it with a wooden toothpick.
- Preheat the Blackstone griddle at medium-high temperature and brush a thin layer of the olive oil on it.
- Cook to desired doneness on the griddle for around 4 to 5 minutes on each side. On buns, serve.

Mexican Burgers

(Preparation time: 10 minutes | Cooking time: 20 minutes | Servings: 5)

Per serving: Calories 536, Total fat 24g, Protein 48g, Carbs 33g

Ingredients:

- 1 plum tomato, diced
- 1 avocado, pitted, peeled & diced
- 1-1/4 lbs. of ground beef
- 1/2 teaspoon of chili powder
- 1-1/4 cup of shredded Pepper Jack cheese
- 2 green onions, chopped
- 3/4 cup to 1 cup of nacho-flavored tortilla chips, crushed
- 1 to 2 teaspoons of lime juice
- Salt and pepper to taste
- 1 egg, beaten
- 1/4 cup of fresh cilantro, chopped
- 1/2 teaspoon of ground cumin
- 5 hamburger buns, split

Instructions:

- Combine avocado, tomato, onions, and lime juice, mash slightly & set aside. In a large-sized mixing bowl, combine the meat, egg, chips, & seasonings. Form into 5 patties.
- Preheat the Blackstone griddle at medium-high temperature and brush a thin layer of the olive oil on it.
- Cook on the griddle for around 4 to 5 minutes on each side till the desired doneness. Add the cheese over burgers and cook the burgers till the cheese has melted. Serve on buns with avocado mixture smeared on top.

Country Friends Chili Burgers

(Preparation time: 10 minutes | Cooking time: 20 minutes | Servings: 4 to 6)

Per serving: Calories 496, Total fat 24g, Protein 39g, Carbs 33g

Ingredients:

- 1 10-1/2 oz. can of condensed bean with bacon soup
- 4 to 6 buns, split and toasted
- 1 lb. of ground beef
- 1 teaspoon of chili powder
- 1/2 cup of catsup

Instructions:

- Preheat the Blackstone griddle at medium-high temperature.
- Place skillet onto the griddle and brown beef in large skillet; drain. Stir in catsup, soup, and chili powder. Let simmer for around 5 to 10 minutes, adding water if more "juice" is desired. Spoon the filling onto the buns and serve.

Dad's Wimpy Burgers

(Preparation time: 10 minutes | Cooking time: 20 minutes | Servings: 6)

Per serving: Calories 633, Total fat 59g, Protein 40g, Carbs 29g

Ingredients:

- 1/2 cup of catsup
- 1 teaspoon of salt
- 6 hamburger buns, split
- 2 lbs. of ground beef
- 1 egg, beaten
- 1 cup of Italian-flavored dry bread crumbs
- 1 onion, chopped

Instructions:

- Combine the meat, catsup, egg, onion, & salt in a large-sized mixing dish and stir well. Make 6–8 patties out of the mixture. In a shallow pan, place bread crumbs. Coat both sides of the patties in crumbs.
- Preheat the Blackstone griddle at medium-high temperature and brush a thin layer of the olive oil on it.
- Place patties on the heated griddle and cook for around 5 to 8 minutes on each side or till lightly browned. On buns, serve.

Simple Chicken Burgers

(Preparation time: 10 minutes | Cooking time: 20 minutes | Servings: 6)

Per serving: Calories 486, Total fat 15g, Protein 16g, Carbs 50g

Ingredients:

- 1 onion, chopped
- 3 tablespoons of chicken broth
- 1 teaspoon of salt-free vegetable seasoning salt
- 1/4 cup of fresh bread crumbs
- 4 to 6 hamburger buns, split
- 1 lb. of ground chicken
- 1/8 teaspoon of garlic powder
- 1 teaspoon of Dijon mustard
- Pepper to taste

Instructions:

- In a large-sized mixing bowl, combine all the ingredients except for the buns. Lightly stir using a fork till everything is well combined. Make 4 to 6 burgers out of the mixture.
- Preheat the Blackstone griddle at medium-high temperature and brush a thin layer of the olive oil on it.
- Place burger patties on the heated griddle. In a skillet, cook burgers for around 6 to 8 minutes on each side, or till no longer pink in the middle. On buns, serve.

Vegetable and Side Dishes Recipes

Marinated Mushroom Kabobs

(Preparation time: 10 minutes | Cooking time: 10 minutes | Servings: 4)

Per serving: Calories 173, Total fat 13g, Protein 3g, Carbs 16g

Ingredients:

- 1 onion, cut into 2-inch pieces
- 1 green pepper, deseeded and cut into 2-inch pieces
- 1-pint of cherry tomatoes
- 1 punnet white button mushrooms, whole
- 1 yellow pepper, deseeded and cut into 2-inch pieces

For the marinade:

- 2 cloves of garlic, minced
- 1/2 teaspoon of dried oregano
- 1/4 cup of olive oil
- 1 lemon, juiced
- 1/2 teaspoon of sea salt

Instructions:

- Arrange vegetables in an alternating pattern on metal skewers.
- Place onto a baking sheet or a piece of aluminum foil to catch the drips.
- In a small-sized mixing bowl, whisk together the marinade ingredients & pour on skewers; turn skewers to coat well.
- Preheat your Blackstone griddle at medium and apply the thin layer of olive oil on the griddle. Cook the steaks for around 4 to 5 minutes on each side till browned.
- Place the kabobs on a serving platter and serve!

Creamy Grilled Potato Salad

(Preparation time: 15 minutes | Cooking time: 10 minutes | Servings: 8)

Per serving: Calories 132, Total fat 9g, Protein 2g, Carbs 14g

Ingredients:

- 2 (1.5 lbs.) bags of baby white potatoes

For the dressing:

- 2 teaspoons of apple cider vinegar
- 1 teaspoon of celery seed
- 1 tablespoon of lemon juice
- ½ teaspoon of sea salt
- ½ cup of mayonnaise
- 1 tablespoon of fresh parsley, chopped
- 1 tablespoon of sour cream
- 2 tablespoons of olive oil
- 1 tablespoon of fresh basil, chopped
- 1 tablespoon of Dijon mustard
- ½ teaspoon of black pepper

Instructions:

- Apply the thin layer of olive oil on the griddle and preheat at medium-high temperature.
- Place potatoes on the griddle and heat for 10 minutes or till tender.
- Remove the potatoes from the griddle and set them aside for 10 minutes to cool.
- In a large-sized mixing bowl, whisk together the dressing ingredients till well blended.

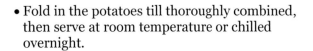

- Fold in the potatoes till thoroughly combined, then serve at room temperature or chilled overnight.

Cumin Chili Potato Wedges

(Preparation time: 10 minutes | Cooking time: 20 minutes | Servings: 4)

Per serving: Calories 343, Total fat 17g, Protein 5g, Carbs 42g

Ingredients:

- 1 teaspoon of cumin
- 3 large russet potatoes, scrubbed and cut into 1-inch-thick wedges
- 1 teaspoon of garlic powder
- 1/3 cup of olive oil
- 1 teaspoon of freshly ground black pepper
- 1 teaspoon of chili powder
- 1 teaspoon of kosher salt

Instructions:

- Set aside a small bowl containing the cumin, chili powder, salt, garlic powder, & pepper.
- Preheat the griddle at medium-high on one side and medium on the other.
- Brush the potatoes all over using olive oil & cook till browned & crisp on both sides, around 2 to 3 minutes per side, on the hot side of the griddle.
- Transfer the potatoes to the cooler side of the grill, cover with foil, and cook for another 5 to 10 minutes, or till cooked through.
- Remove the potatoes out from the griddle and place them in a large-sized mixing dish. Toss the vegetables in the spice mixture to coat them.
- Serve them warm and enjoy it.

Grilled Corn

(Preparation time: 10 minutes | Cooking time: 15 minutes | Servings: 8)

Per serving: Calories 343, Total fat 17g, Protein 5g, Carbs 42g

Ingredients:

- 1/2 stick of butter, unsalted
- 8 ears corn, shucked & rinsed
- Sea salt, to taste

Instructions:

- Preheat your Blackstone griddle for 10 minutes at medium-high temperature.
- Spray the griddle using non-stick cooking spray and cook the corn directly on it, regularly flipping, till charred on all sides and thoroughly cooked, about 10 minutes.
- Remove the corn from the griddle & set aside for 2 minutes to cool.
- Roll in butter, season using salt, and serve immediately.

Parmesan-Garlic Asparagus

(Preparation time: 10 minutes | Cooking time: 10 minutes | Servings: 6)

Per serving: Calories 108, Total fat 8g, Protein 6g, Carbs 4g

Ingredients:

- 2 tablespoons of olive oil
- Sea salt, to taste
- 1 pound of fresh asparagus
- 3 tablespoons of parmesan cheese, shaved
- Black pepper, to taste
- 2 garlic cloves, minced

Instructions:

- Preheat your Blackstone griddle at a medium-high temperature. Apply a thin layer of olive oil on the griddle.
- Remove the bottoms of the asparagus spears.
- Toss the asparagus with the olive oil and season using salt & pepper on a baking sheet.
- Cook the asparagus in a row on the griddle for around 5 to 10 minutes, till char marks appear, and they are tender when probed with a fork.
- Toss the asparagus with the garlic and parmesan on the baking pan and serve warm.

Zucchini in pink pepper and parsley mustard

(Preparation time: 10 minutes | Cooking time: 10 minutes | Servings: 4)

Per serving: Calories 90, Total fat 2g, Protein 4g, Carbs 9g

Ingredients:

- 1 tablespoon of parsley leaves
- Salt and pepper to taste
- 2.2. lbs. of zucchinis
- Olive oil to taste
- 1 tablespoon of pink peppercorns
- 3 tablespoons of mustard

Instructions:

- Peel & wash zucchinis before slicing them lengthwise into thin slices.
- For direct cooking, preheat the Blackstone griddle at 390°F.
- Brush some oil on the griddle.
- Season the zucchinis using salt and black pepper after brushing them with oil.
- Cook the zucchinis for 3 minutes on each side of the griddle.
- Place the zucchinis on a serving dish after removing them from the griddle.
- Oil & pink peppercorns are used to season.
- Parsley leaves should be washed and chopped in the meantime.
- Place the mustard in a mixing bowl.
- Combine the parsley and mustard in a mixing dish and stir thoroughly.
- The zucchinis are now ready to be served with the parsley mustard.

Avocado and cheddar potatoes

(Preparation time: 10 minutes | Cooking time: 25 minutes | Servings: 4)

Per serving: Calories 360, Total fat 12g, Protein 10g, Carbs 31g

Ingredients:

- 1 cup of cheddar cheese
- Salt and pepper to taste
- 8 Medium potatoes
- 2 sprigs of rosemary
- 1/2 cup of cubed avocado
- 4 tablespoons of olive oil

Instructions:

- Peel the potatoes, carefully wash them, and afterward cut them into slices.
- The rosemary should be washed and dried.
- Remove the central stone from the avocado and wash the pulp & cube.
- Cutting the cheddar cheese into the cubes.
- Brush a baking tray using a small amount of oil.
- Sprinkle the potatoes with cheddar cheese and place them in the bottom of the pan.
- After that, toss in the avocado cubes.
- Preheat your Blackstone griddle at 400°F for indirect cooking in the meantime.
- In a baking pan, combine all of the ingredients.
- Cook for around 20 minutes on the Blackstone griddle.
- Check for doneness, and if necessary, continue cooking for another 5 minutes.
- Take them out of the griddle as soon as they're done, place them on serving plates, and serve

Halloumi and Tomatoes in Balsamic Vinegar

(Preparation time: 10 minutes | Cooking time: 35 minutes | Servings: 4)

Per serving: Calories 210, Total fat 10g, Protein 19g, Carbs 11g

Ingredients:

- 1 sprig of thyme
- 20 cherry tomatoes
- Balsamic vinegar to taste
- 1/2 cup of cubed halloumi cheese
- Olive oil to taste
- 1 tablespoon of chopped pistachios
- Salt and pepper to taste

Instructions:

- Prepare your Blackstone griddle at (450°F) for indirect cooking.
- In the meantime, wash and rinse the cherry tomatoes before halving them.
- Take the cherry tomatoes and place them in the roasting pan.
- The thyme & sage should be washed and dried before being chopped.
- Thyme should be sprinkled over the tomatoes.
- Add the halloumi cheese cubes last.
- Place on the Blackstone griddle and season using oil, salt, & pepper.
- Allow tomatoes and halloumi to simmer for around 35 minutes at 450°F.
- Remove them and place them on plates, and serve.
- Serve over tomatoes with a drizzle of balsamic vinegar & chopped pistachios.

Grilled Tzatziki Feta

(Preparation time: 10 minutes | Cooking time: 35 minutes | Servings: 4)

Per serving: Calories 190, Total fat 9g, Protein 18g, Carbs 14g

Ingredients:

- 1 tablespoon of dried oregano
- Salt and pepper to taste
- 6 oz. of cubed feta
- Olive oil to taste
- 1 sprig of thyme
- Tzatziki sauce to taste

Instructions:

- Prepare your Blackstone griddle at 450°F for indirect cooking.
- The thyme & sage should be washed and dried before being chopped.
- Oregano & other aromatic herbs should be sprinkled over the cubed feta.
- Place on the Blackstone griddle and season using oil, salt, and pepper.
- Cook the feta for around 35 minutes.
- Take it out of the griddle when it's done, plate it, and serve.

- Serve with a dollop of tzatziki sauce on top.

Easy Fried Rice

(Preparation time: 10 minutes | Cooking time: 10 minutes | Servings: 2)

Per serving: Calories 557, Total fat 20g, Protein 14g, Carbs 49g

Ingredients:

- 2 large eggs
- 2 tablespoons of olive oil
- 4 cups of rice, cooked
- 2 tablespoons of green onion, sliced
- 1 teaspoon of salt

Instructions:

- Whisk eggs in a bowl and set aside.
- Preheat your Blackstone griddle at medium-high.
- Coat the top of the griddle using cooking spray.
- Cook till cooked rice separates from each other on a heated griddle top.
- Rice should be pushed to one side of the griddle top. Pour the beaten egg into the griddle with the oil.
- Add salt and quickly mix the egg with the rice, cooking till the rice grains are completely covered by the egg.
- Stir in the green onion for around 2 minutes.
- Enjoy and serve.

Healthy Zucchini Noodles

(Preparation time: 10 minutes | Cooking time: 10 minutes | Servings: 4)

Per serving: Calories 124, Total fat 8g, Protein 3g, Carbs 11g

Ingredients:

- 1 tablespoon of soy sauce
- 2 tablespoons olive oil
- 4 small zucchinis, spiralized

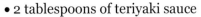

- 2 tablespoons of teriyaki sauce
- 2 onions, spiralized
- 1 tablespoon of sesame seeds

Instructions:

- Preheat your Blackstone griddle at medium-high.
- Oil the top of the heated griddle.
- Sauté for around 4-5 minutes after adding the onion.
- Cook for around 2 minutes after adding the zucchini noodles.
- Cook for around 4-5 minutes with teriyaki sauce, sesame seeds, and soy sauce.
- Enjoy and serve.

Stir Fry Vegetables

(Preparation time: 10 minutes | Cooking time: 20 minutes | Servings: 4)

Per serving: Calories 218, Total fat 13g, Protein 3g, Carbs 25g

Ingredients:

- 1/4 cup of olive oil
- 2 medium parsnips, peeled & cut into small pieces
- 2 medium potatoes, cut into small pieces
- Black pepper & salt to taste
- 3 medium carrots, peeled & cut into small pieces
- 1 small rutabaga, peeled & cut into small pieces

Instructions:

- Preheat your Blackstone griddle at medium-high.
- Toss veggies using olive oil in a large-sized mixing dish.
- Transfer the vegetables to a hot griddle top & stir-fried till they're soft.
- Enjoy your servings.

Easy Seared Green Beans

(Preparation time: 10 minutes | Cooking time: 10 minutes | Servings: 6)

Per serving: Calories 100, Total fat 5g, Protein 3g, Carbs 12g

Ingredients:

- 1 1/2 tablespoons of rice vinegar
- 1 1/2 tablespoons of sesame oil
- 1 1/2 lbs. of green beans, trimmed
- 1 1/2 tablespoons of brown sugar
- 3 tablespoons of soy sauce
- 2 tablespoons of sesame seeds, toasted
- 1/4 teaspoon of black pepper

Instructions:

- Green beans should be cooked for around 3 minutes in boiling water and then drained properly.
- Drain the green beans and return them to the cold ice water. Green beans should be patted dry.
- Preheat your Blackstone griddle at medium-high.
- Oil the top of the heated griddle.
- Stir in the green beans for around 2 minutes.
- Stir in the soy sauce, vinegar, brown sugar, and pepper for another 2 minutes.
- Toss in the sesame seeds and coat thoroughly.
- Enjoy and serve.

Italian Zucchini Slices

(Preparation time: 10 minutes | Cooking time: 10 minutes | Servings: 4)

Per serving: Calories 125, Total fat 12g, Protein 2g, Carbs 4g

Ingredients:

- 2 garlic cloves, minced
- 1 tablespoon of fresh lemon juice
- 2 zucchinis, cut into 1/2-inch-thick slices
- 1 1/2 tablespoons of fresh parsley, chopped
- Salt and pepper to taste
- 1 teaspoon of Italian seasoning
- 1/4 cup of butter, melted

Instructions:

- Melted butter, lemon juice, pepper, Italian seasoning, garlic, & salt are combined in a small bowl.
- Brush the melted butter mixture over the zucchini slices.
- Preheat your Blackstone griddle at medium-high.
- Cook zucchini slices for around 2 minutes on each side on the griddle top.
- Serve the zucchini slices on a dish with parsley on top.
- Enjoy your servings.

Polenta with Rosemary

(Preparation time: 10 minutes | Cooking time: 10 minutes | Servings: 6)

Per serving: Calories 71, Total fat 1g, Protein 2g, Carbs 16g

Ingredients:

- 2 teaspoons extra-virgin olive oil
- Lemon pepper to taste
- 24-oz. log prepared polenta
- 2 tablespoons of chopped rosemary
- Garlic salt to taste

Instructions:

- Preheat your Blackstone griddle at high. The polenta should be cut into 1/2-inch-thick pieces. On a baking sheet, arrange the slices.
- Brush both sides of the polenta rounds using olive oil, then season with lemon pepper, garlic salt, and chopped rosemary leaves. Using a brush, lightly oil the grill rack.
- Grill the polenta pieces on the griddle for around 3 to 5 minutes per side, or till beautifully browned. Remove from the griddle and serve immediately on a warmed plate.

Mediterranean Grilled Broccoli

(Preparation time: 10 minutes | Cooking time: 10 minutes | Servings: 6)

Per serving: Calories 106, Total fat 10g, Protein 2g, Carbs 5g

Ingredients:

- 1 1/2 teaspoons of garlic, minced
- 4 tablespoons of olive oil
- 4 cups of broccoli florets
- 1 tablespoon of lemon juice
- 1 1/4 teaspoons of kosher salt
- 1 1/2 teaspoons of Italian seasoning
- 1/4 teaspoon of pepper

Instructions:

- In a large-sized mixing dish, combine the broccoli and the remaining ingredients. Refrigerate for 1 hour after covering with plastic wrap. Preheat your griddle at a high temperature.
- Coat the top of the griddle with cooking spray. Cook broccoli florets for around 3 minutes on each side on a heated griddle top. Serve and have fun.

Spinach Salad with Tomato Melts

(Preparation time: 10 minutes | Cooking time: 10 minutes | Servings: 4)

Per serving: Calories 121, Total fat 15g, Protein 8g, Carbs 17g

Ingredients:

- 2 tablespoons of good-quality olive oil, plus more for brushing
- 1 teaspoon of Dijon mustard
- 1 or 2 large fresh tomatoes (enough for 4 thick slices across)
- 6 slices of cheddar cheese (about 4 ounces)
- Salt and pepper
- 3 cups of baby spinach
- 2 teaspoons of white wine vinegar

Instructions:

- Save the trimmings after you've cored the tomatoes & cut 4 thick slices (approximately 1 inch). Brush them with oil and season them on both sides using salt and pepper.
- In a mixing bowl, combine the 2 tablespoons of oil, vinegar, & mustard. Chop the tomato trimmings and toss them with the spinach in the dressing till everything is uniformly coated.
- Preheat your griddle grill at medium-high. Allow the griddle to heat till the oil is shimmering, but it is not smoking. Cook for around 3 minutes with the tomato slices.
- Flip the tomatoes, top every slice with a piece of cheddar, and cook for another 2 to 3 minutes, or till the cheese is melted. Place the salad on top of the plates and serve.

Parmesan and Garlic Potatoes

(Preparation time: 10 minutes | Cooking time: 55 minutes | Servings: 4)

Per serving: Calories 308, Total fat 4g, Protein 5g, Carbs 34g

Ingredients:

- 1 tablespoon of seeds oil
- 4 Medium potatoes
- 1 tablespoon of parmesan
- Salt and pepper to taste
- 1 tablespoon of chopped garlic clove
- 1 teaspoon of oregano

Instructions:

- Wash the potatoes underneath running water first.
- Boil potatoes for around 30 minutes or till fork-tender in salted water.
- Allow potatoes to cool completely before draining.
- Meanwhile, peel and finely cut 1 tablespoon of garlic clove.
- Combine olive oil, salt, parmesan, garlic, and black pepper in a mixing bowl.
- Cut the chilled potatoes into quarters & toss lightly with the garlic and parmesan mixture.
- Fill a baking pan halfway with potatoes and the rest of the ingredients in the bowl.

- Preheat your Blackstone griddle at 400°F in one zone.
- Place the baking pan on the griddle & cook for around 15 minutes on indirect heat.
- Check to see whether they're done and if they aren't, cook for another 5 minutes.
- Remove them from the griddle as soon as they're done and serve right away.

Provolone and Leeks Eggs

(Preparation time: 10 minutes | Cooking time: 20 minutes | Servings: 4)

Per serving: Calories 325, Total fat 20g, Protein 19g, Carbs 14g

Ingredients:

- 1/4 cup of whole meal breadcrumbs
- Salt and pepper to taste
- 2 cups of leeks
- 1 tablespoon of grated Parmesan cheese
- 4 eggs
- Olive oil to taste
- 1/2 cup of provolone cheese

Instructions:

- Clean the leeks first.
- Leeks should be cut off at the root, then cut horizontally and leafed through.
- After washing them underneath running water, boil them into salted water for around 10 minutes.
- Drain them and set them aside to cool.
- Brush a baking dish using olive oil before sprinkling it with breadcrumbs.
- Place a layer of leeks on top, followed by a layer of provolone slices.
- Continue in this manner till all the ingredients have been used.
- Now add the oil, salt, and pepper to taste.
- Preheat your Blackstone griddle for around 15 minutes at 446°F (direct cooking).
- Place the grill on high and place the baking dish in the center. Cook for around 10 minutes.

- Place the eggs on top of the leeks after 10 minutes, sprinkle with Parmesan cheese, and simmer for another 6 minutes.
- Remove the pan from the griddle and set it aside for 5 minutes to cool.
- Serve by dividing the leeks & eggs into four parts and plating them on plates.

Poultry Recipes

- 1 tablespoon of olive oil, 1/4 teaspoon of salt, and 1/4 teaspoon of pepper, evenly sprinkled on chicken
- Cook around 5 minutes on each side or till a meat thermometer inserted in the thickest piece registers 165°F after spraying the griddle with nonstick cooking spray.
- Allow for 5 minutes of rest before cutting into slices.
- In a large-sized mixing bowl, combine the remaining 3 tablespoons of oil, vinegar, remaining 1/2 teaspoon of salt, honey, mustard, & the remaining 1/4 teaspoon of pepper. Toss in the spinach, basil, & onion gently to coat.
- To serve, divide the salad between two plates and top evenly with the chicken, blackberries, & cheese.

Basil, Blackberry, and Grilled Chicken Salad

(Preparation time: 10 minutes | Cooking time: 20 minutes | Servings: 2)

Per serving: Calories 607, Total fat 40g, Protein 48g, Carbs 16g

Ingredients:

- 1/4 cup of extra-virgin olive oil, divided
- 1 1/2 teaspoons of honey
- 1/2 teaspoon of black pepper, divided
- 2 boneless, skinless chicken breasts,
- 4 cups of baby spinach
- 1 punnet of fresh blackberries
- 3/4 teaspoon of kosher salt, divided
- 2 cups of fresh basil, stems removed
- 2 tablespoons of white balsamic vinegar
- 1 1/2 teaspoons of Dijon mustard
- Cooking spray
- 1/4 cup of red onion, super-thinly sliced
- ½ cup of goat cheese, crumbled

Instructions:

- Preheat your griddle at medium-high temperature.

Chicken Thighs with Ginger-Sesame Glaze

(Preparation time: 10 minutes | Cooking time: 20 minutes | Servings: 4 to 8)

Per serving: Calories 301, Total fat 11g, Protein 43g, Carbs 5g

Ingredients:

- 8 boneless and skinless chicken thighs

For the glaze:

- 1 tablespoon of fresh garlic, minced
    - ⅓ cup of scallions, thinly sliced
- 3 tablespoons of dark brown sugar
- 1 teaspoon of fresh ginger, minced
- 2 1/2 tablespoons of soy sauce
- Non-stick cooking spray
- 2 teaspoons of sesame seeds
- 1 teaspoon of sambal oelek

Instructions:

- In a large-sized mixing dish, combine glaze ingredients; separate and set aside half for serving.
- Toss the chicken in the dish to evenly coat it.

- Preheat your griddle at a medium-high temperature.
- Spray the pan using cooking spray.
- Cook for around 6 minutes on each side or till chicken is cooked through.
- To serve, transfer the chicken to plates & sprinkle with the remaining glaze.

Lemon-Olive Grilled Chicken

(Preparation time: 20 minutes | Cooking time: 20 minutes | Servings: 4)

Per serving: Calories 166, Total fat 5g, Protein 23g, Carbs 4g

Ingredients:

- 1 shallot, chopped
- 1 lb. of chicken breast tenders

For the marinade:

- 1 teaspoon of lemon zest
- ½ teaspoon of white pepper
- 1 lemon, juiced
- ¼ cup of white wine, like Chardonnay
- 4 teaspoons of olive oil
- 1 teaspoon of sugar
- ½ teaspoon of sea salt

Instructions:

- In a mixing dish, combine the marinade ingredients; after thoroughly blended, add the chopped shallot & chicken to coat well.
- Refrigerate for 30 minutes after covering and marinating.
- Preheat your griddle at medium-high temperature. Cook for around 7 minutes per side on the griddle, or till a meat thermometer reads 165°F.
- After cooking, let the chicken rest for around 5 minutes before serving with your favorite sides.

Lemon Ginger Chicken with Fruit Salsa

(Preparation time: 10 minutes | Cooking time: 25 minutes | Servings: 3)

Per serving: Calories 479, Total fat 26g, Protein 45g, Carbs 16g

Ingredients:

- 1 bag (8 oz.) of romaine salad
- 3 boneless chicken breast halves
- 1 cup of strawberries, sliced
- Sea salt for seasoning
- 1/4 cup of poppy seed dressing, plus ½ cup for basting chicken
- 1 cup of fresh blueberries, rinsed
- Black pepper, for seasoning
- 1/4 cup of almonds, sliced

Instructions:

- Take 1/2 cup of poppy seed dressing and baste the chicken. Using a pinch of pepper & sea salt, season each chicken breast.
- Preheat your griddle at medium-high temperature.
- Grill chicken for around 10 minutes on each side or till no longer pink in the center, brushing with additional poppy seed dressing as needed.
- Allow five minutes for the chicken to rest.
- Combine the lettuce mix and the remaining 1/4 cup of dressing.
- Divide the salad among three bowls and top with an equal amount of blueberries & strawberries in each.
- Chicken should be cut crosswise into 1/2-inch-thick slices.
- To serve, place one sliced chicken breast in each salad bowl and top with almonds.

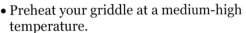

Korean Grilled Chicken Wings with Scallion

(Preparation time: 20 minutes | Cooking time: 40 minutes | Servings: 6)

Per serving: Calories 312, Total fat 13g, Protein 44g, Carbs 2g

Ingredients:

- 2 pounds of chicken wings (flats & drumettes attached or separated)

For the marinade:

- 1 teaspoon of sea salt, plus more
- 1/2 cup of gochujang, Korean hot pepper paste
- 1 scallion, thinly sliced, for garnish
- 1 tablespoon of olive oil
- 1/2 teaspoon of black pepper

Instructions:

- After rinsing the wings, blot them dry using paper towels.
- In a large-sized mixing bowl, whisk together all of the marinade ingredients till thoroughly incorporated.
- Toss the wings in the dish to coat them.
- Refrigerate for 30 minutes after wrapping the bowl with plastic wrap.
- One side of the griddle should be set at medium temperature, while the other should be set at medium-high.
- Working in batches, cook wings over medium temperature for about 12 minutes, regularly flipping, till the skin begins to brown.
- Transfer wings to a medium-high region of the griddle and char for around 5 minutes on each side, or till cooked through; a meat thermometer should read 165°F when touched to the bone.
- Serve the wings heated with your preferred dipping sauces on a plate with scallions on top.

Yellow Curry Chicken Wings

(Preparation time: 20 minutes | Cooking time: 40 minutes | Servings: 6)

Per serving: Calories 324, Total fat 14g, Protein 46g, Carbs 2g

Ingredients:

- 2 lbs. of chicken wings

For the marinade:

- 1 tablespoon of mild yellow curry powder
- ½ teaspoon of sea salt
- 1 teaspoon of red chili flakes
- 1/2 cup of Greek yogurt, plain
- 1 tablespoon of olive oil
- ½ teaspoon of black pepper

Instructions:

- After rinsing the wings, blot them dry using paper towels.
- In a large-sized mixing bowl, whisk together all of the marinade ingredients till thoroughly incorporated.
- Toss the wings in the dish to coat them.
- Refrigerate for 30 minutes after wrapping the bowl with plastic wrap.
- One side of the griddle should be set to medium temperature, while the other should be set to medium-high.
- Working in batches, griddle wings over medium temperature for about 12 minutes, regularly flipping, till the skin begins to brown.
- Transfer wings to a medium-high region of the griddle and char for around 5 minutes on each side, or till cooked through; a meat thermometer should read 165°F when touched to the bone.
- Transfer the wings to a serving plate and keep them warm.

Buffalo Grilled Chicken Wings

(Preparation time: 10 minutes | Cooking time: 20 minutes | Servings: 6 to 8)

Per serving: Calories 410, Total fat 21g, Protein 49g, Carbs 4g

Ingredients:

- 1 teaspoon of ground black pepper
- 1/3 cup of buffalo sauce
- 1 tablespoon of sea salt
- 3 lbs. of chicken wings
- 1 tablespoon of honey
- 1 teaspoon of garlic powder
- 6 tablespoons of unsalted butter
- 1 tablespoon of apple cider vinegar

Instructions:

- In a large-sized mixing bowl, combine the salt, pepper, & garlic powder.
- To coat the wings, toss them in the spice mixture.
- Preheat your griddle at medium-high temperature.
- Place the wings on the griddle, touching them to keep the meat juicy on the bone during grilling.
- For a total of 20 minutes of cooking, flip the wings every 5 minutes.
- In a saucepan over low flame, melt the butter and mix in the buffalo sauce, vinegar, & honey.
- Toss the wings in a large-sized mixing dish with the sauce to coat them.
- Return the wings to the griddle over medium-high temperature and cook till the skins are crisp, around 1 to 2 minutes on each side.
- To serve, return the wings to the bowl with the sauce & toss to combine.

Chicken Wings with Sweet Red Chili and Peach Glaze

(Preparation time: 15 minutes | Cooking time: 30 minutes | Servings: 4)

Per serving: Calories 790, Total fat 17g, Protein 66g, Carbs 47g

Ingredients:

- 1 cup of sweet red chili sauce
- 1 tablespoon of fresh cilantro, minced
- 1 jar of peach preserves (12 oz.)
- Non-stick cooking spray
- 1 teaspoon of lime juice
- 1 bag of chicken wing sections (2-1/2 lbs.)

Instructions:

- In a mixing bowl, combine the preserves, red chili sauce, lime juice, & cilantro. Cut in half and set aside one half for serving.
- Preheat your griddle at medium and coat it using nonstick cooking spray.
- Cook the wings for around 25 minutes, frequently rotating till the juices flow clear.
- Remove the wings from the griddle and toss them in a bowl with the remaining glaze.
- Return the wings to the griddle and cook for around 3 to 5 minutes more, flipping once.
- Serve with your favorite dips & side dishes while still warm!

California Grilled Chicken

(Preparation time: 20 minutes | Cooking time: 20 minutes | Servings: 4)

Per serving: Calories 883, Total fat 62g, Protein 55g, Carbs 30g

Ingredients:

- 2 tablespoons of extra virgin olive oil
- 1 teaspoon of oregano
- 4 boneless and skinless chicken breasts
- 1 teaspoon of garlic powder
- 3/4 cup of balsamic vinegar
- 1 tablespoon of honey
- 1 teaspoon of basil

For the garnish:

- 4 slices of fresh mozzarella cheese
- Sea salt
- 4 slices of beefsteak tomato
- Black pepper, fresh ground
- Balsamic glaze for drizzling
- 4 slices of avocado

Instructions:

- In a large-sized mixing bowl, combine balsamic vinegar, basil, honey, olive oil, oregano, and garlic powder.
- Toss in the chicken to coat & refrigerate for 30 minutes.

- Preheat your griddle at medium-high temperature. Cook for around 7 minutes per side on the griddle, or till a meat thermometer reads 165°F.
- Top each chicken breast in mozzarella, avocado, & tomato and cook for around 2 minutes, tenting with foil to melt.
- Drizzle with balsamic glaze & season with a pinch of salt & black pepper.

Honey Balsamic Marinated Chicken

(Preparation time: 20 minutes | Cooking time: 20 minutes | Servings: 4)

Per serving: Calories 485, Total fat 18g, Protein 66g, Carbs 11g

Ingredients:

- 1/2 teaspoon of sea salt
- 2 lbs. of boneless and skinless chicken thighs
- 1/2 teaspoon of paprika
- 1 teaspoon of olive oil
- 3/4 teaspoon of onion powder
- 1/4 teaspoon of black pepper

For the Marinade:

- 2 tablespoons of balsamic vinegar
- 1 teaspoon of garlic, minced
- 2 tablespoons of honey
- 2 tablespoons of tomato paste

Instructions:

- In a sealable plastic bag, combine the chicken, olive oil, paprika, salt, black pepper, & onion powder. Set aside after sealing and tossing the chicken to coat it in spices and oil.
- Combine the balsamic vinegar, garlic, tomato paste, & honey in a mixing bowl.
- Dividing the marinade in half is a good idea. Combine one half with the chicken bag and put the other half in the refrigerator in a covered container.
- Toss the chicken in the bag to coat it. Refrigerate for 30 to 4 hours before serving.
- Preheat your griddle at medium-high temperature.

- Remove the bag from the marinade and throw it away. Cook for 7 minutes per side on the griddle, or till juices flow clear & a meat thermometer reads 165°F.
- Brush the remaining marinade over the top of chicken thighs during the last minute of cooking.
- Serve right away.

Classic BBQ Chicken

(Preparation time: 10 minutes | Cooking time: 1 hour 30 minutes | Servings: 4 to 6)

Per serving: Calories 539, Total fat 12g, Protein 87g, Carbs 15g

Ingredients:

- Olive oil
- 4 pounds of chicken, including the legs, thighs, wings, & breasts, skin-on
- 1 cup of barbecue sauce
- Salt

Instructions:

- Rub the chicken using salt and olive oil.
- Preheat your griddle at medium-high.
- Grill the chicken skin side down for 5-10 minutes.
- Reduce the temperature to medium-low & cook for 30 minutes, tenting the griddle with foil.
- Turn the chicken over and baste with the remaining barbecue sauce.
- Allow for another 20 minutes of cooking time after re-covering the chicken.
- Baste, cover, and cook for another 30 minutes, basting and turning once more.
- Once the internal temperature of the chicken pieces reaches 165°F and the juices run clear, the chicken is done.
- To serve, baste with extra barbecue sauce.

Honey Herb Chicken Tenders

(Preparation time: 10 minutes | Cooking time: 10 minutes | Servings: 4)

Per serving: Calories 467, Total fat 21g, Protein 50g, Carbs 19g

Ingredients:

- 1 teaspoon of dried oregano
- 2 tablespoons of olive oil
- 1/3 cup of Dijon mustard
- 1 1/2 lbs. of chicken tenders
- 2 tablespoons of Herb de province
- 1 shallot, minced
- Salt & pepper to taste
- 1 teaspoon of dried rosemary
- 2 tablespoons of lemon juice
- 4 tablespoons of honey

Instructions:

- In a zip-lock bag, combine the chicken and the additional ingredients. Refrigerate overnight after sealing the bag & shaking it well.
- Preheat your griddle at medium-high.
- Coat the top of the griddle using cooking spray.
- Cook for around 5 minutes on each side on a hot griddle top with marinated chicken tenders.
- Enjoy your meal.

Ranch Chicken Patties

(Preparation time: 10 minutes | Cooking time: 10 minutes | Servings: 4)

Per serving: Calories 404, Total fat 22g, Protein 44g, Carbs 2g

Ingredients:

- 1 cup of cheddar cheese, shredded
- 2 tablespoons of ranch seasoning mix
- 1 lb. of ground chicken
- 1/3 cup of bacon, cooked & chopped

Instructions:

- In a mixing bowl, combine all of the ingredients and stir till well blended.
- Preheat your griddle at medium-high.
- Coat the top of the griddle with cooking spray.

- Make patties using the ingredients and cook for around 5 minutes on each side onto a hot griddle.
- Enjoy your meal.
-

14. Spicy Chicken

(Preparation time: 10 minutes | Cooking time: 10 minutes | Servings: 4)

Per serving: Calories 281, Total fat 12g, Protein 34g, Carbs 8g

Ingredients:

- 2 bell peppers, cut into 1-inch pieces
- 1/2 teaspoon of chili powder
- 1/2 teaspoon of onion powder
- 1 lb. of chicken breasts, boneless & cut into 1-inch pieces
- 1 teaspoon of paprika
- 1 tablespoon of olive oil
- 1 onion, cut into 1-inch pieces
- 1/2 teaspoon of garlic powder
- 1/2 teaspoon of pepper
- 1 teaspoon of salt
- 1/2 teaspoon of oregano

Instructions:

- In a mixing dish, combine the chicken and the remaining ingredients.
- Preheat your griddle at medium-high.
- Coat the top of the griddle using cooking spray.
- Place the chicken mixture on a hot griddle & cook for around 8-10 minutes, or till the chicken is fully cooked.
- Enjoy your meal.

Chicken with Pesto

(Preparation time: 10 minutes | Cooking time: 10 minutes | Servings: 4)

Per serving: Calories 537, Total fat 37g, Protein 49g, Carbs 3g

Ingredients:

- 1/3 cup of olive oil
- 4 chicken breasts, boneless & skinless
- 2 tablespoons of lemon juice
- Salt and pepper to taste
- 1/3 cup of parmesan cheese, grated
- 2 cups of baby spinach
- 1 teaspoon of lemon zest
- 1/4 cup of pine nuts, toasted

Instructions:

- Season the chicken using salt and pepper.
- Preheat your griddle at medium-high.
- Coat the top of the griddle using cooking spray.
- Cook the chicken for around 5 minutes on each side on a hot griddle.
- In a blender, combine all of the remaining ingredients, except for the cheese, and blend till smooth.
- Combine the blended mixture and the cheese in a mixing bowl.
- Serve with a dollop of pesto on top of the roasted chicken.

Lemon Honey Chicken

(Preparation time: 10 minutes | Cooking time: 15 minutes | Servings: 4)

Per serving: Calories 261, Total fat 9g, Protein 33g, Carbs 10g

Ingredients:

- 2 tablespoons of honey
- 4 lemon juice
- 1 lb. of chicken breasts, boneless
- 1 tablespoon of Dijon mustard
- Salt and pepper to taste

Instructions:

- Toss together the chicken, honey, pepper, mustard, lemon juice, & salt in a mixing bowl. Allow 12 hours for marinating.
- Preheat your griddle at medium-high.
- Coat the top of the griddle using cooking spray.

- Cook the chicken for around 6-8 minutes on each side onto a hot griddle.
- Enjoy your meal.

Spicy Chicken Thighs

(Preparation time: 10 minutes | Cooking time: 15 minutes | Servings: 4)

Per serving: Calories 619, Total fat 49g, Protein 43g, Carbs 4g

Ingredients:

- 1 tablespoon of ground pepper
- 4 chicken thighs
- 2 garlic cloves, minced
- 4 thyme sprigs, chopped
- Salt and pepper to taste
- 3/4 cup of olive oil
- 1/2 small shallot, diced
- 2 rosemary sprigs, chopped
- 1 cup of parsley, chopped

Instructions:

- In a zip-lock bag, combine the chicken and the additional ingredients. Refrigerate for 8 hours after sealing the bag and shaking it firmly.
- Preheat your griddle at medium-high.
- Coat the top of the griddle using cooking spray.
- Cook the marinated chicken for around 7-8 minutes on each side onto a hot griddle.
- Enjoy your meal.

Tex Mex Chicken

(Preparation time: 10 minutes | Cooking time: 15 minutes | Servings: 4)

Per serving: Calories 285, Total fat 13g, Protein 34g, Carbs 10g

Ingredients:

- 2 tablespoons of brown sugar
- 1/4 teaspoon of ground cloves
- 1 lb. of chicken breasts, boneless

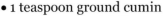

- 1 teaspoon ground cumin
- 1 tablespoon of chili powder
- 1 tablespoon of olive oil
- 1/2 teaspoon of pepper
- 1/2 teaspoon of salt
- 1/2 teaspoon of garlic powder
- 1/4 teaspoon of red chili flakes
- 2 teaspoons of onion powder
- 2 tablespoons of lime juice
- 1 teaspoon of dried oregano
- 1 teaspoon of paprika

Instructions:

- In a zip-lock bag, combine the chicken and the additional ingredients. Refrigerate for 1 hour after sealing the bag and shaking it well.
- Preheat your griddle at medium-high.
- Coat the top of the griddle using cooking spray.
- Cook the marinated chicken for around 5-6 minutes on each side on a hot griddle.
- Enjoy your meal.

Marinated Buttermilk Chicken

(Preparation time: 10 minutes | Cooking time: 15 minutes | Servings: 4)

Per serving: Calories 325, Total fat 16g, Protein 36g, Carbs 8g

Ingredients:

- 2 tablespoons of butter, melted
- 1 teaspoon of onion powder
- 1 lb. of chicken breasts, boneless
- 1/2 teaspoon of chili powder
- Salt & pepper to taste
- 1 tablespoon of garlic, minced
- 1 tablespoon of brown sugar
- 1 1/2 cups of buttermilk
- 2 teaspoons of Italian seasoning

Instructions:

- In a zip-lock bag, combine the chicken and the additional ingredients. Refrigerate overnight after sealing the bag and shaking it well.
- Preheat your griddle at medium-high.
- Coat the top of the griddle using cooking spray.

- Cook the marinated chicken for around 4-5 minutes on each side onto a hot griddle.
- Enjoy your meal.

Perfect Greek Chicken

(Preparation time: 10 minutes | Cooking time: 15 minutes | Servings: 4)

Per serving: Calories 314, Total fat 19g, Protein 33g, Carbs 4g

Ingredients:

- 1 tablespoon of red wine vinegar
- 1 tablespoon of garlic, minced
- 1 lb. of chicken breasts, boneless & skinless
- 1/2 teaspoon of dried oregano
- Salt & pepper to taste
- 3 tablespoons of olive oil
- 1/2 teaspoon of dried rosemary
- 3 tablespoons of lemon juice
- 1/2 teaspoons of dried thyme

Instructions:

- In a zip-lock bag, combine the chicken and the additional ingredients. Refrigerate overnight after sealing the bag and shaking it well.
- Preheat your griddle at medium-high.
- Coat the top of the griddle using cooking spray.
- Cook the marinated chicken for around 5-6 minutes on each side onto a hot griddle.
- Enjoy your meal.

Easy Blackened Chicken

(Preparation time: 10 minutes | Cooking time: 10 minutes | Servings: 4)

Per serving: Calories 266, Total fat 14g, Protein 33g, Carbs 2g

Ingredients:

- 2 tablespoons of blackened seasoning
- 1 lb. of chicken breasts, boneless and skinless
- 2 tablespoons of butter, melted

Instructions:

- Rub melted butter and spice all over the chicken.
- Preheat your griddle at medium-high.
- Coat the top of the griddle using cooking spray.
- Cook the chicken for around 4-5 minutes on each side onto a hot griddle.
- Enjoy your meal.

Flavorful Italian Chicken

(Preparation time: 10 minutes | Cooking time: 15 minutes | Servings: 4)

Per serving: Calories 378, Total fat 16g, Protein 50g, Carbs 6g

Ingredients:

- 1 tablespoon of olive oil
- 2 tablespoons of dried thyme
- 1 1/2 lbs. of chicken breasts, boneless & skinless
- 2 tablespoons of garlic powder
- Salt & pepper to taste
- 2 tablespoons of dried basil
- 2 tablespoons of dried oregano

Instructions:

- Combine the oil, basil, garlic powder, pepper, thyme, oregano, and salt in a small-sized bowl.
- Brush the olive oil mixture over the chicken breasts.
- Preheat your griddle at medium-high.
- Cook the chicken for around 5-7 minutes on each side onto a hot griddle.
- Enjoy your meal.

Turkey Recipes

Smoked Young Turkey

(Preparation time: 20 minutes | Cooking time: 2 hours 10 minutes | Servings: 6)

Per serving: Calories 240, Total fat 9g, Protein 15g, Carbs 27g

Ingredients:

- 6 glasses of olive oil with roasted garlic flavor
- 1 fresh or thawed frozen young turkey
- 6 original Yang dry lab or the poultry seasonings

Instructions:

- Turkey breasts & cavities should be free of extra fat and skin.
- Slowly peel the turkey skin away from the breast and a portion of the leg, leaving skin intact.
- Olive oil should be used on the chest, underneath the skin, and on the skin.
- Rub or season the chest cavity, underneath the skin, and on the skin gently.
- Preheat your Blackstone griddle at medium temperature for indirect cooking.
- Place the turkey meat, chest up, on the griddle.
- Suck the turkey for around 1 to 2 hours, or till the thickest section of the turkey's chest hits 170°F, and the liquid is clear.
- Place the turkey in a loose foil tent for around 20 minutes before engraving.

Smokey Whole Turkey

(Preparation time: 20 minutes | Cooking time: 2 hours | Servings: 10)

Per serving: Calories 146, Total fat 8g, Protein 18g, Carbs 4g

Ingredients:

- 2 tablespoons of chopped fresh parsley
- 1 frozen whole turkey, giblets removed, thawed
- 1 teaspoon of ground black pepper
- 1 cup of butter, unsalted, softened, divided
- 2 tablespoons of orange zest
- 1 teaspoon of salt
- ½ cup of water
- 2 tablespoons of chopped fresh rosemary
- 14.5-ounces of chicken broth
- 2 tablespoons of chopped fresh sage
- 2 tablespoons of chopped fresh thyme

Instructions:

- Preheat your griddle at 180°F till the green light on the dial blinks, indicating that the griddle has attained the desired temperature.
- In the meantime, prepare the turkey by tucking its wings under it using kitchen twine.
- In a dish, combine parsley, 1/2 cup of butter, thyme, sage, orange zest, & rosemary; stir well to combine; brush generously on the interior and outside of the turkey; season the external of the turkey with salt & black pepper.
- Place the turkey breast side up in a roasting pan, pour in the stock & water, add the remaining butter, then place the pan on the griddle.
- Cook for around the turkey for 1 hour, then raise the temperature at 350°F and cook for another 1 hour, or till the turkey is well cooked, and the internal temperature reaches 165°F, basting the chicken with the drippings every 30 minutes but not in the last hour.
- Remove the roasting pan out from the griddle and set it aside for around 20 minutes to allow the turkey to rest.
- Carve the turkey into serving pieces.

Thanksgiving Turkey

(Preparation time: 20 minutes | Cooking time: 3 hours | Servings: 6)

Per serving: Calories 278, Total fat 31g, Protein 22g, Carbs 4g

Ingredients:

- 2 teaspoons of kosher salt
- 2 cups of butter (softened)
- 2 tablespoons of freshly chopped parsley
- 6 garlic cloves (minced)
- 1 tablespoon of cracked black pepper
- 2 teaspoons of dried thyme
- 2 tablespoons of freshly chopped rosemary
- 1 (around 18 pounds) turkey
- 2 tablespoons of freshly chopped sage

Instructions:

- Combine butter, 1 teaspoon of black pepper, thyme, sage, rosemary, parsley, 1 teaspoon of salt, & garlic in a mixing bowl.
- To loosen out the skin out from the turkey, use your fingers.
- Generously, Rub the butter mixture beneath the skin of the turkey and all over it.
- Season the turkey liberally with the herb mixture.
- Preheat your griddle at 300°F for 15 minutes with the lid closed.
- Place your turkey on the griddle & cook for around 3 hours, or till the temperature of the turkey thigh reaches 160°F.
- Remove the turkey flesh from the griddle & set it aside to cool. Cut into serving sizes and portions.

Savory-Sweet Turkey Legs

(Preparation time: 10 minutes | Cooking time: 3 hours | Servings: 4)

Per serving: Calories 190, Total fat 9g, Protein 24g, Carbs 5g

Ingredients:

- ¼ cup of packed light brown sugar
- 1-gallon of hot water
- 1 teaspoon of ground cloves
- 4 turkey legs
- 1 cup of curing salt
- 1 teaspoon of freshly ground black pepper
- 2 teaspoons of liquid smoke
- Mandarin Glaze, for serving
- 1 bay leaf

Instructions:

- Stir together the water, pepper, curing salt, brown sugar, bay leaf, cloves, and liquid smoke in a large container with a lid till the salt and sugar are dissolved; set aside to come to room temperature.
- Refrigerate the turkey legs overnight after submerging them in the seasoned brine.
- Remove the turkey legs out from the brine & rinse them before cooking; discard the brine.
- Get your griddle ready. Preheat it at 225°F. Apply a thin layer of oil on the griddle.
- Place the turkey legs on the griddle, cover, & cook for around 2 to 3 hours, or till dark brown and 165°F on a meat thermometer inserted into the thickest portion of the meat.
- Serve with a side of Mandarin Glaze or poured on top of the turkey legs.

Brined Turkey Breast

(Preparation time: 10 minutes | Cooking time: 3 hours | Servings: 6)

Per serving: Calories 250, Total fat 5g, Protein 18g, Carbs 31g

Ingredients:

For the Brine:

- 2 tablespoons of ground black pepper
- 1 cup of brown sugar
- 2 pounds of turkey breast, deboned
- 4 cups of cold water
- ¼ cup of salt

For the BBQ Rub:

- 2 tablespoons of ground black pepper

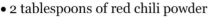

- 2 tablespoons of red chili powder
- 2 tablespoons of garlic powder
- 2 tablespoons of sugar
- 2 tablespoons of dried onions
- 2 tablespoons of ground cumin
- ¼ cup of paprika
- 2 tablespoons of brown sugar
- 1 tablespoon of salt
- 1 tablespoon of cayenne pepper

Instructions:

- Prepare the brine by combining black pepper, salt, and sugar in a large-sized mixing dish, then adding water and stirring till the sugar has dissolved.
- Place the turkey breast in it, immerse it well, and refrigerate it for at least 12 hours.
- Meanwhile, make the BBQ rub by combining all of the ingredients in a small-sized bowl and stirring till well blended. Set aside till needed.
- After that, take the turkey breast out of the brine & season generously with Prepare BBQ rub.
- Once you're ready to cook, turn on the griddle, set the temperature at 180°F, and wait at least 15 minutes for it to warm.
- When the griddle has reached temperature, open the lid, set the turkey breast on the griddle grate and cook for around 2 to 3 hours, or till the internal temp reaches 160°F.
- Transfer the turkey to a cutting board and set it aside for 10 minutes before cutting it into slices.

Turkey Legs

(Preparation time: 10 minutes | Cooking time: 3 hours | Servings: 4)

Per serving: Calories 216, Total fat 13g, Protein 69g, Carbs 5g

Ingredients:

- 4 turkey legs
For the Brine:

- ½ cup of brown sugar
- 2 teaspoons of liquid smoke

- ½ cup of curing salt
- 4 cups of ice
- 1 tablespoon of whole black peppercorns
- 8 cups of cold water
- 1 cup of BBQ rub
- 2 bay leaves
- 16 cups of warm water

Instructions:

- To make the brine, fill a large stockpot halfway with heated water, add the peppercorns, bay leaves, & liquid smoke, toss in the salt, sugar, & BBQ seasoning, and bring to the boil.
- Remove the saucepan from the flame and allow it to cool to room temperature before adding cold water, ice cubes, and chilling the brine in the refrigerator.
- Then put the turkey legs in it, completely submerge them, and refrigerate for 24 hours.
- Remove the turkey legs out from the brine after 24 hours, rinse thoroughly, and pat dry using paper towels.
- When you're ready to cook, turn on the griddle, adjust the temperature at 250°F, and wait at least 15 minutes for it to warm. Apply a thin layer of oil on the griddle.
- When the griddle is hot, remove the cover, set the turkey legs on the griddle and cook for around 1 to 2 hours, or till the internal temp hits 165°F. Serves right away.

Herb Roasted Turkey

(Preparation time: 15 minutes | Cooking time: 2 hours 30 minutes | Servings: 12)

Per serving: Calories 155, Total fat 4g, Protein 29g, Carbs 8g

Ingredients:

- 2 tablespoons of chopped mixed herbs
- ¼ teaspoon of ground black pepper
- 14 pounds of turkey, cleaned
- 8 tablespoons of butter, unsalted, softened
- Pork and poultry rub as needed
- 2 cups of chicken broth
- 3 tablespoons of butter, unsalted and melted

Instructions:

- Remove the giblets from the turkey, wash it inside and out, then wipe it dry using paper towels before placing it on a roasting pan & tucking the turkey wings with butcher's thread.
- Preheat your griddle for a minimum of 15 minutes by turning it on and setting the temperature at 325°F.
- Meanwhile, make herb butter by placing melted butter in a small-sized bowl, adding black pepper & mixed herbs, and whisking till frothy.
- Using the handle of a wooden spoon, put some of the Prepare herb butter below the skin of the turkey and massage the skin to properly spread the butter.
- After that, spread melted butter all over the turkey's exterior, season using pork and poultry rub, & pour the liquid into the roasting pan.
- When the griddle is hot, remove the cover, lay the roasting pan with the turkey on the griddle and cook for around 2 hours and 30 minutes, or till the internal temperature reaches 165°F & the top is golden brown.
- Transfer the turkey to a chopping board and set aside for 30 minutes before carving it into slices & serve.

Mexican Turkey Patties

(Preparation time: 15 minutes | Cooking time: 10 minutes | Servings: 4)

Per serving: Calories 237, Total fat 13g, Protein 32g, Carbs 4g

Ingredients:

- 1 tablespoon of taco seasoning
- 1 lb. of ground turkey
- 1/2 cup of green peppers, chopped
- Salt & pepper to taste
- 1/2 cup of red peppers, chopped

Instructions:

- In a mixing bowl, combine all of the ingredients and stir till well blended.

- Preheat your griddle at medium-high temperature and apply a thin layer of oil on the griddle.
- Coat the top of the griddle using cooking spray.
- Make patties using the ingredients & cook for around 4-5 minutes on each side on a hot griddle.
- Enjoy your meal.

Spinach Turkey Patties

(Preparation time: 10 minutes | Cooking time: 10 minutes | Servings: 12)

Per serving: Calories 244, Total fat 13g, Protein 32g, Carbs 3g

Ingredients:

- 5 cups of spinach, sautéed
- 3 lbs. of ground turkey
- Salt & pepper to taste
- 3 tablespoons of garlic, minced
- 3 tablespoons of mustard
- 1 onion, chopped

Instructions:

- In a mixing bowl, combine all of the ingredients & stir till well blended.
- Preheat your griddle at medium-high. Apply a thin layer of oil on the griddle.
- Coat the top of the griddle using cooking spray.
- Make patties using the ingredients & cook for around 5 minutes on each side on a hot griddle.
- Enjoy your meal.

Turkey Sandwich

(Preparation time: 10 minutes | Cooking time: 10 minutes | Servings: 1)

Per serving: Calories 307, Total fat 16g, Protein 23g, Carbs 16g

Ingredients:

- 3 oz. of turkey breast, cooked and shredded
- 1 cheese slice
- 2 bread slices

- 1 tablespoon of mayonnaise

Instructions:

- On one side of each bread slice, spread mayonnaise.
- Top 1 slice of bread with turkey & cheese
- Cover with the last slice of bread.
- Preheat your griddle at medium-high. Apply a thin layer of oil on the griddle.
- Coat the top of the griddle using cooking spray.
- Cook the sandwich for around 5 minutes on a heated griddle top or till golden brown on both sides.
- Enjoy your meal.

Smoked Cheese and Raw Ham Turkey Rolls

(Preparation time: 15 minutes | Cooking time: 15 minutes | Servings: 4)

Per serving: Calories 310, Total fat 14g, Protein 36g, Carbs 4g

Ingredients:

- 8 slices of raw ham
- Salt & pepper to taste
- 1 turkey breast of 14 oz.
- Olive oil to taste
- 8 slices of smoked cheese

Instructions:

- Start by removing any excess fat or bone fragments from the turkey breasts.
- Wash & dry the turkey breast before slicing it horizontally into four pieces using the meat tenderizer and putting them in baking paper.
- Take a piece of turkey and pack it with two slices of smoked cheese, two slices of raw ham, and then roll it over itself.
- Preheat your Blackstone griddle at 390°F (direct cooking) for around 10 minutes.
- Arrange the rolls on the griddle evenly spaced so that you can easily turn them.
- Cook for around 4 minutes, then use the barbeque tongs to rotate them to 90 degrees and cook for another 4 minutes on each side, for a total of around 16 minutes.

- Remove them and set them on a serving platter.
- Allow the meat to rest for a few minutes before serving.

BBQ Turkey Legs

(Preparation time: 15 minutes | Cooking time: 2 hours | Servings: 4)

Per serving: Calories 643, Total fat 37g, Protein 73g, Carbs 4g

Ingredients:

- 4 turkey legs

For the Brine:

- ½ cup of brown sugar
- ½ cup of curing salt
- 16 cups of warm water
- 2 bay leaves
- 1 tablespoon of whole black peppercorns
- 8 cups of cold water
- 1 cup of BBQ rub
- 2 teaspoons of liquid smoke
- 4 cups of ice

Instructions:

- To make the brine, fill a large stockpot halfway with heated water, add the peppercorns, bay leaves, & liquid smoke, toss in the sugar, salt, and BBQ seasoning, and bring to the boil.
- Remove the saucepan from the flame and allow it to cool to room temperature before adding cold water, ice cubes, & chilling the brine in the refrigerator.
- Then put the turkey legs in it, completely submerge them, and refrigerate for 24 hours.
- Remove the turkey legs from the brine after 24 hours, rinse thoroughly, and pat dry using paper towels.
- Preheat your Blackstone griddle at 250°F and apply a thin layer of oil on the griddle.
- When the griddle is hot, set the turkey legs on the griddle and cook for around 2 hours. Flip the legs halfway through the cooking.
- Serve right away.

Grilled Apple Turkey

(Preparation time: 10 minutes | Cooking time: 3 hours | Servings: 6)

Per serving: Calories 369, Total fat 14g, Protein 46g, Carbs 14g

Ingredients:

- ¼ cup of poultry seasoning
- 2 teaspoons of dried sage
- 1 (12-pound/5 kg) of turkey, giblets removed
- ½ cup of apple juice
- Extra-virgin olive oil for rubbing
- 2 teaspoons of dried thyme
- 8 tablespoons (1 stick) of unsalted butter, melted

Instructions:

- Preheat your Blackstone griddle at 250°F.
- Inside and out, rub the turkey using oil and season with the poultry seasoning, getting beneath the skin.
- For basting, combine the sage, melted butter, apple juice, and thyme in a bowl.
- Place the turkey in a roasting pan on the griddle, cover, and cook for around 2 to 3 hours, basting every hour, or till a meat thermometer placed in the thickest part of thigh hits 165°F.
- Allow around 15 to 20 minutes for the turkey to rest before cutting.

Rub Seasoned Turkey

(Preparation time: 10 minutes | Cooking time: 2 hours | Servings: 14)

Per serving: Calories 715, Total fat 38g, Protein 107g, Carbs 4g

Ingredients:

- 2 tablespoons of olive oil
- 1 whole turkey
- 1 batch of Chicken Rub

Instructions:

- Preheat your griddle at 350°F.
- Arrange the turkey on its breast on a work surface to remove the backbone. Cut down one side of the turkey's backbone, then the other, using kitchen shears. Remove the bone.
- Flip the turkey breast-side up & flatten it once the backbone has been removed.
- Brush the turkey using olive oil and season it with the rub on both sides. Work the rub into the flesh and skin using your hands.
- Place the turkey, breast-side up, directly on the griddle and cook till the internal temp hits 170°F.
- Before carving and serving, remove the turkey from the griddle and let it rest for 10 minutes.

Honeyed Barbecue Turkey

(Preparation time: 10 minutes | Cooking time: 30 minutes | Servings: 4)

Per serving: Calories 364, Total fat 21g, Protein 32g, Carbs 11g

Ingredients:

- 1 tablespoon of Worcestershire sauce
- 2 tablespoons pf regular BBQ sauce
- 1 teaspoon of garlic, crushed
- 2 tablespoons of honey bourbon BBQ sauce
- 4 turkey breasts
- ¼ cup of olive oil
- 1 tablespoon of sweet mesquite seasoning
- 2 tablespoons of spicy BBQ sauce

Instructions:

- Preheat your griddle at medium temperature and apply a thin layer of oil to the griddle.
- Combine the garlic, oil, Worcestershire sauce, & mesquite seasoning in a large mixing bowl.
- Evenly coat the chicken breasts in the spice mixture.
- Cook for around 20-30 minutes on the griddle with the chicken breasts.
- Meanwhile, combine all three BBQ sauces in a mixing bowl.
- Coat the breasts with the BBQ sauce mixture in the last 4-5 minutes of cooking. Serve immediately.

Grilled Pepper Turkey Breast

(Preparation time: 10 minutes | Cooking time: 2 hours | Servings: 4)

Per serving: Calories 377, Total fat 14g, Protein 57g, Carbs 4g

Ingredients:

- Freshly ground black pepper, to taste
- 1 (around 3-pounds/ 1.3 kg) turkey breast
- 1 teaspoon of garlic powder
- Salt, to taste

Instructions:

- Preheat your Blackstone griddle at 180°F and apply a thin layer of oil on it.
- Season both sides of the turkey breast using salt, pepper, & garlic powder.
- Put the breast on the griddle and cook for around 1 hour.
- Raise the temperature of the griddle at 350°F & continue to cook till the internal temperature of the turkey reaches 170°F. Take the breast off the griddle and serve right away.

Authentic BBQ Turkey

(Preparation time: 10 minutes | Cooking time: 2 hours | Servings: 8)

Per serving: Calories 403, Total fat 25g, Protein 27g, Carbs 18g

Ingredients:

- 2 teaspoons of ground black pepper
- 2 cups of The Ultimate BBQ Sauce or your preferred barbecue sauce, divided
- 8 boneless and skinless chicken breasts
- 2 teaspoons of salt
- 2 teaspoons of garlic powder

Instructions:

- Preheat your Blackstone griddle at 250°F.
- Sprinkle the salt, pepper, & garlic powder on both sides of the turkey breasts in a big pan, making sure to work the seasonings in beneath the skin.

- Put the roasting pan on the griddle, cover, and cook for around 1 hour 30 minutes to 2 hours, or till a meat thermometer placed into the thickest portion of each breast registers 165°F. Top the turkey using 1 cup of barbecue sauce for the final 15 minutes of cooking.
- With the leftover 1 cup of barbecue sauce, serve the turkey warm.

Espresso Drizzled Barbecue Chicken

(Preparation time: 10 minutes | Cooking time: 2 hours | Servings: 4)

Per serving: Calories 323, Total fat 10g, Protein 40g, Carbs 15g

Ingredients:

- 1 tablespoon of chili powder
- 2 tablespoons of olive oil
- 1 tablespoon of brown sugar
- ½ tablespoon of ground espresso
- 1 tablespoon of lime zest
- ½ cup of barbecue sauce
- ½ teaspoon of ground cumin
- Salt, to taste
- 8 turkey legs

Instructions:

- Combine the sugar, lime zest, espresso powder, chili powder, cumin, & salt in a mixing bowl. Drizzle some oil over the turkey legs.
- Using a pastry brush, coat the chicken in the sugar mixture. Refrigerate for around 5 hours after covering with foil.
- Preheat your Blackstone griddle at 180°F.
- Cook the turkey legs for around 1 hour. Raise the temperature at 350° F.
- Cook the chicken legs for a further hour on the griddle, flipping once. Brush the turkey using barbecue sauce and cook for a further 10 minutes on the griddle.

Nutritious Roasted Turkey

(Preparation time: 10 minutes | Cooking time: 2 hours 30 minutes | Servings: 12)

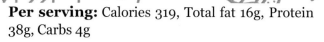

Per serving: Calories 319, Total fat 16g, Protein 38g, Carbs 4g

Ingredients:

- ¼ teaspoon of ground black pepper
- 4 pounds of turkey (1.8 kg), cleaned
- 8 tablespoons of butter, unsalted, softened
- 2 tablespoons of chopped mixed herbs
- 2 cups of chicken broth
- Pork & poultry rub, as needed
- 3 tablespoons of butter, unsalted, melted

Instructions:

- Remove the giblets from the turkey, wash it inside and out, then wipe it dry using paper towels before placing it on a roasting pan, then tucking the turkey wings with butcher's thread.
- Preheat your Blackstone griddle at 350°F.
- Meanwhile, make herb butter by placing melted butter in a small-sized bowl, adding black pepper & mixed herbs, and whisking till frothy.
- Using the handle of a wooden spoon, place some of the created herb butter beneath the skin of the turkey and massage the skin to evenly spread the butter.
- After that, spread melted butter all over the turkey's exterior, season using pork and poultry rub, & pour the liquid into the roasting pan.
- When the griddle is hot, lay the roasting pan with the turkey on the griddle and cook for around 2 hours and 30 minutes, or till the internal temp hits 165°F and the top is golden brown.
- When the turkey is done, take it to a cutting board and let it rest for 30 minutes before carving it into slices and serving it.

Worcestershire Turkey Legs

(Preparation time: 10 minutes | Cooking time: 3 hours | Servings: 6)

Per serving: Calories 217, Total fat 7g, Protein 36g, Carbs 5g

-

Ingredients:

For the Turkey:

- 1 tablespoon of canola oil
- 3 tablespoons of Worcestershire sauce
- 6 turkey legs

For the Rub:

- 1 tablespoon of brown sugar
- ¼ cup of chipotle seasoning
- 1 tablespoon of paprika

For the Sauce:

- 1 tablespoon of canola oil
- 1 cup of white vinegar
- 1 tablespoon of chipotle BBQ sauce

Instructions:

- Combine the Worcestershire sauce & canola oil in a mixing bowl for the turkey.
- Loosen the skin on your legs using your fingers.
- Apply the oil mixture on the undersides of the legs using your fingers.
- Combine the ingredients for the rubs in a separate bowl.
- Apply a large amount of the spice mixture to the underside and outside surface of the turkey legs.
- Refrigerate for 2-4 hours after placing the legs in a large sealable bag.
- Before cooking, remove the turkey legs from the refrigerator and allow them to come to room temperature for approximately 30 minutes.
- Preheat your griddle at 250°F for around 15 minutes.
- In a small-sized saucepan, combine all sauce ingredients and simmer over low flame, constantly stirring, till completely warmed.
- Arrange the turkey legs on the griddle and cook for around 2 to 3 hours, basting every 45 minutes with sauce.
- Serve immediately.

Pork Recipes

- Remove the plastic wrap from the pork & make a lengthwise incision through the center of the tenderloin, opening the meat so it sits flat but not all the way through.
- In a small-sized mixing bowl, combine tapenade & parmesan; rub into the tenderloin's center and fold flesh back together.
- Using twine, tie the pieces together at 2-inch intervals.
- Sear tenderloin for around 20 minutes, or till the internal temperature reaches 145°F, flipping once while cooking.
- The tenderloin should be placed on a cutting board.
- Cover with foil and set aside for 10 minutes.
- Remove the string and cut the pieces into 1/4-inch thick slices to serve.

Herb-Crusted Mediterranean Pork Tenderloin

(Preparation time: 10 minutes | Cooking time: 30 minutes | Servings: 4)

Per serving: Calories 413, Total fat 30g, Protein 31g, Carbs 3g

Ingredients:

- 1 tablespoon of olive oil
- 1 teaspoon of garlic powder
- 1 pound of pork tenderloin
- 3 tablespoons of olive tapenade
- 2 teaspoons of dried oregano
- ¼ cup of parmesan cheese, grated
- 3/4 teaspoon of lemon pepper

Instructions:

- Place the pork on a big plastic wrap sheet.
- Oil the tenderloin and evenly sprinkle garlic powder, oregano, & lemon pepper on the entire tenderloin.
- Refrigerate for around 2 hours after wrapping tightly in plastic wrap.
- Heat your Blackstone griddle at medium-high. Apply a thin layer of oil on the griddle.

Paprika Dijon Pork Tenderloin

(Preparation time: 10 minutes | Cooking time: 4 hours | Servings: 6)

Per serving: Calories 484, Total fat 25g, Protein 51g, Carbs 14g

Ingredients:

- 2 tablespoons of Dijon mustard
- 1 teaspoon of salt
- 2 1 lb. pork tenderloins
- 2 tablespoons of olive oil
- 1 1/2 teaspoons of smoked paprika

Instructions:

- Combine the mustard & paprika in a small-sized bowl.
- Preheat your Blackstone griddle at medium. Apply a thin layer of oil on the griddle.
- Make sure the tenderloins are evenly coated with the mustard mixture.
- Cook the tenderloins on the griddle till nicely browned on all sides and the internal temperature reaches 135°F.
- Before slicing and serving, remove the tenderloins out from the griddle and let them rest for 5 minutes.

Grilled Pork Chops with Herb Apple Compote

(Preparation time: 10 minutes | Cooking time: 20 minutes | Servings: 4)

Per serving: Calories 284, Total fat 20g, Protein 18g, Carbs 7g

Ingredients:

- 1 teaspoon of chopped fresh rosemary
- 4, bone-in pork chops
- Black pepper
- 2 honey crisp apples, peeled, cored and chopped
- Sea salt
- 1/3 cup of orange juice
- 1 teaspoon of chopped fresh sage

Instructions:

- In a saucepan, combine the apples, herbs, & orange juice and cook, occasionally stirring, till the apples are soft and the juices have thickened to a thin syrup, around 10 to 12 minutes.
- Pork chops should be seasoned using salt and black pepper.
- Preheat your Blackstone griddle at medium-high temperature and apply a thin layer of oil on the griddle.
- Place the pork chop on the griddle and cook for around 4 minutes, till it releases from the griddle.
- Cook for another 3 minutes on the other side.
- Tent with foil and move to a cutting board.
- Serve with apple compote on top!

Glazed Country Ribs

(Preparation time: 10 minutes | Cooking time: 3 hours | Servings: 6)

Per serving: Calories 404, Total fat 8g, Protein 60g, Carbs 15g

Ingredients:

- ¼ cup of onion, finely chopped
- 2 tablespoons of Worcestershire sauce
- 3 pounds of country-style pork ribs
- 2 cloves of garlic, minced
- 2 teaspoons of chili powder
- 1 cup of low-sugar ketchup
- ½ cup of water
- ¼ cup of light molasses
- ¼ cup of cider vinegar or wine vinegar

Instructions:

- In a saucepan, combine ketchup, vinegar, water, onion, chili powder, molasses, Worcestershire sauce, & garlic; bring to the boil. Cook, frequently stirring, for around 10 to 15 minutes, or till desired thickness is reached, uncovered.
- Trim out all the fat from ribs.
- Preheat your griddle at medium-high temperature. Apply a thin layer of oil on the griddle.
- Place the ribs on the griddle, bone-side down, and cook for around 1 1/2 to 2 hours, or till tender, brushing using sauce every 10 minutes during the very last 10 minutes of cooking.
- Enjoy the remaining sauce and serve!

Garlic Soy Pork Chops

(Preparation time: 20 minutes | Cooking time: 1-hour | Servings: 4 to 6)

Per serving: Calories 398, Total fat 38g, Protein 14g, Carbs 4g

Ingredients:

- 1/2 cup of olive oil
- 4 to 6 pork chops
- 1/2 teaspoon of salt
- 4 cloves of garlic, finely chopped
- 1/2 cup of soy sauce
- 1/4 cup of butter
- 1/2 teaspoon of garlic powder
- 1/2 teaspoon of black pepper

Instructions:

- Combine the garlic, soy sauce, olive oil, & garlic powder in a big zip lock bag. Place the pork

chops in the marinade and ensure they are well coated. Allow 30 minutes for preparation.
- Preheat your griddle at medium-high. Add two tablespoons of oil and two tablespoons of butter to the griddle.
- Place the chops on the griddle one at a time, being careful not to crowd them. Cook the chops for around 5 minutes on the griddle with additional 2 tablespoons of butter. Cook for another 4 minutes.
- Remove the chops out from the griddle and brush them with the remaining butter. After 5 minutes of resting, serve.

Soy Honey Pork Chops

(Preparation time: 20 minutes | Cooking time: 25 minutes | Servings: 6)

Per serving: Calories 251, Total fat 9g, Protein 30g, Carbs 13g

Ingredients:

- 1/4 cup of organic honey
- 2 tablespoons of olive oil
- 6 (4 ounces) of boneless pork chops
- 1 to 2 tablespoons of low sodium soy sauce
- 1 tablespoon of rice mirin

Instructions:

- Whisk together the honey, oil, soy sauce, & white vinegar till completely blended. In a big sealable plastic bag, combine the sauce and pork chops & marinate for 1 hour.
- Preheat your griddle at medium-high & cook the pork chop for around 4 to 5 minutes, or till it easily slides off the griddle.
- Cook for around 5 minutes more on the other side, or till the internal temperature has reached 145°F.
- Enjoy your meal!

Cuban Pork Chops

(Preparation time: 20 minutes | Cooking time: 1 hour 30 minutes | Servings: 4)

Per serving: Calories 323, Total fat 27g, Protein 18g, Carbs 3g

Ingredients:

- 4 cloves of garlic, smashed
- 1/3 cup of lime juice
- 1 teaspoon of ground cumin
- 4 pork chops
- 2 tablespoons of olive oil
- 1/4 cup of water
- Salt & black pepper

Instructions:

- Preheat the griddle at medium temperature. Cook the pork chops till they are lightly browned on both sides after sprinkling salt on them.
- In a mixing dish, whisk together the water, garlic, & lime juice till smooth.
- Continue to cook the pork chops in the lime juice mixture while basting them.
- Remove the pork chops out from the griddle when done cooking and garnish with more sauce & black pepper before serving.

Spicy Cajun Pork Chops

(Preparation time: 10 minutes | Cooking time: 15 minutes | Servings: 4)

Per serving: Calories 320, Total fat 26g, Protein 18g, Carbs 3g

Ingredients:

- 1/2 teaspoon of black pepper
- 1/2 teaspoon of ground cumin
- 4 pork chops
- 1 tablespoon of butter
- 1/2 teaspoon of dried sage
- 1 tablespoon of paprika
- 1/4 teaspoon of cayenne pepper
- 1 tablespoon of vegetable oil
- 1/2 teaspoon of salt
- 1/2 teaspoon of garlic powder

Instructions:

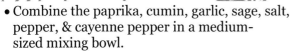

- Combine the paprika, cumin, garlic, sage, salt, pepper, & cayenne pepper in a medium-sized mixing bowl.
- Heat the oil and butter in a griddle at medium-high temperature.
- Season the pork chops generously using the spice rub.
- Cook for around 4 to 5 minutes on the griddle with the chops. Cook for another 4 minutes after turning the pork chops.
- Allow 5 minutes for the pork chops to rest after removing them from the griddle.

Marinated Pork Chops

(Preparation time: 10 minutes | Cooking time: 10 minutes | Servings: 4)

Per serving: Calories 351, Total fat 27g, Protein 19g, Carbs 6g

Ingredients:

- 1 teaspoon of garlic, minced
- 4 pork chops
- 1/3 cup of Worcestershire sauce
- 1/4 teaspoon of cayenne
- 2 tablespoons of olive oil
- 1/2 teaspoon of pepper
- Salt
- 1/4 cup of soy sauce
- 1/3 cup of balsamic vinegar

Instructions:

- In a zip-lock bag, combine the pork chops and the additional ingredients. Refrigerate for around 4 hours after sealing the bag and shaking it firmly.
- Preheat your griddle at medium-high temperature.
- Coat the top of the griddle using cooking spray.
- Place the marinated pork chops onto a hot griddle top & cook for around 3-5 minutes on each side, or till the internal temperature reaches 145°F.
- Enjoy your meal.

Delicious Boneless Pork Chops

(Preparation time: 10 minutes | Cooking time: 15 minutes | Servings: 4)

Per serving: Calories 299, Total fat 20g, Protein 19g, Carbs 10g

Ingredients:

- 4 pork chops, boneless

For the rub:

- 1/2 teaspoon of ground cumin
- 1 teaspoon of pepper
- 1 tablespoon of sugar
- 1/2 teaspoon of ground ginger
- 2 tablespoons of brown sugar
- 1 1/2 tablespoons of paprika
- 1/2 teaspoon of dry mustard
- 1 teaspoon of garlic powder

Instructions:

- Mix pork chops & rub ingredients thoroughly in a mixing dish.
- Preheat your griddle at medium-high.
- Coat the top of the griddle using cooking spray.
- Place pork chops on a heated griddle top & cook for around 6 minutes on each side or till the internal temperature reaches 145°F.
- Enjoy your meal.

Flavors Balsamic Pork Chops

(Preparation time: 10 minutes | Cooking time: 15 minutes | Servings: 4)

Per serving: Calories 360, Total fat 31g, Protein 18g, Carbs 2g

Ingredients:

- 1/8 teaspoon of chili flakes
- 4 pork chops
- 2 tablespoons of Dijon mustard
- 1/2 cup of balsamic vinegar
- 1 teaspoon of dried rosemary
- 1/2 teaspoon of pepper
- 3/4 teaspoon of salt

- 1 teaspoon of garlic, minced
- 3 tablespoons of olive oil

Instructions:

- In a zip-lock bag, combine the pork chops and the additional ingredients. Refrigerate for around 4 hours after sealing the bag and shaking it firmly.
- Preheat your griddle at medium-high temperature.
- Coat the top of the griddle using cooking spray.
- Place the marinated pork chops on a heated griddle top & cook for around 6-8 minutes on each side, or till the internal temperature has reached 145°F.
- Enjoy your meal.

Pineapple Honey Pork Chops

(Preparation time: 10 minutes | Cooking time: 15 minutes | Servings: 4)

Per serving: Calories 351, Total fat 20g, Protein 19g, Carbs 25g

Ingredients:

- 1 tablespoon of Dijon mustard
- 1 cup of crushed pineapple
- 4 pork chops, boneless
- Salt & pepper to taste
- 1/4 cup of honey

Instructions:

- In a zip-lock bag, combine the pork chops and the additional ingredients. Refrigerate overnight after sealing the bag and shaking it well.
- Preheat your griddle at medium-high.
- Coat the top of the griddle using cooking spray.
- Cook pork chops for around 5-6 minutes on each side on a heated griddle top.
- Enjoy your meal.

Herb Pork Chops

(Preparation time: 10 minutes | Cooking time: 15 minutes | Servings: 6)

Per serving: Calories 306, Total fat 20g, Protein 18g, Carbs 13g

Ingredients:

- 6 pork chops

For the brine:

- 1 tablespoon of coriander seeds
- 2 thyme sprigs
- 1 tablespoon of peppercorns
- 2 bay leaves
- Salt
- 1 tablespoon of juniper berries
- 1/2 cup of demerara sugar

Instructions:

- Bring 1 liter of water and all of the brine ingredients to the boil in a pot. Remove the saucepan from the flame and let the brine to cool completely.
- Put the pork chops in the brine for 2 hours to marinate.
- Preheat your griddle at medium-high.
- Coat the top of the griddle using cooking spray.
- Cook pork chops for around 4-5 minutes on each side on a heated griddle top.
- Enjoy your meal.

Dijon Pork Skewers

(Preparation time: 10 minutes | Cooking time: 15 minutes | Servings: 4)

Per serving: Calories 628, Total fat 40g, Protein 50g, Carbs 16g

Ingredients:

- 2 cups of cherry tomatoes
- 1 1/2 lbs. of pork loin, cut into 1-inch cubes
- 2 cups of bell peppers, cut into pieces
- 2 cups of mushrooms
- 2 cups of onion, cut into pieces

For the marinade:

- 1/4 cup of Dijon mustard

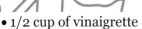

- 1/2 cup of vinaigrette
- Salt & ground black pepper

Instructions:

- Mix the pork cubes with the marinade ingredients in a mixing bowl & set aside for around 30 minutes to marinate.
- Using skewers, thread marinated pork cubes, onion, mushrooms, tomatoes, and bell peppers.
- Preheat your griddle at medium-high.
- Cook skewers for around 5-7 minutes on each side or till cooked through on a hot griddle top.
- Enjoy your meal.

Moist Pork Chops

(Preparation time: 10 minutes | Cooking time: 15 minutes | Servings: 4)

Per serving: Calories 373, Total fat 33g, Protein 19g, Carbs 2g

Ingredients:

- 2 tablespoons of soy sauce
- 4 pork chops
- 1/4 cup of olive oil
- 2 teaspoons of Montreal marinade

Instructions:

- Mix the pork chops with the remaining ingredients in a mixing bowl and set aside for around 6 hours to marinate.
- Preheat your griddle at medium-high.
- Coat the top of the griddle using cooking spray.
- Cook pork chops for around 5-7 minutes on each side on a heated griddle top.
- Enjoy your meal.

Pork Patties

(Preparation time: 10 minutes | Cooking time: 15 minutes | Servings: 4)

Per serving: Calories 85, Total fat 2g, Protein 15g, Carbs 2g

Ingredients:

- 1/2 teaspoon of onion powder
- 1 lb. of ground pork
- 1/2 teaspoon of dried thyme
- 3/4 teaspoon of fennel seeds
- 1/8 teaspoon of red pepper, crushed
- 1 teaspoon of garlic powder
- 3/4 teaspoon of pepper
- 1/2 teaspoon of salt
- 1/8 teaspoon of ground nutmeg
- 3/4 teaspoon of ground sage

Instructions:

- In a mixing bowl, combine all of the ingredients & stir till well blended.
- Preheat your griddle at medium-high.
- Coat the top of the griddle using cooking spray.
- Make patties using the ingredients & cook for around 5 minutes on each side on a hot griddle.
- Enjoy your meal.

Pork Pineapple Skewers

(Preparation time: 10 minutes | Cooking time: 15 minutes | Servings: 4)

Per serving: Calories 307, Total fat 14g, Protein 32g, Carbs 11g

Ingredients:

- 1 lime juice
- 1 lb. of pork fillet, cut into chunks
- 1 teaspoon of ground allspice
- 2 cups of pineapple cubes
- 1 tablespoon of hot sauce
- 2 tablespoons of Creole seasoning

Instructions:

- Mix together the pork, pineapple cubes, hot sauce, lime juice, allspice, & spices in a mixing dish.
- Preheat your griddle at medium-high.
- Coat the top of the griddle using cooking spray.
- Using skewers, thread pork & pineapple chunks.

- Cook the skewers on a hot griddle till the pork is done.
- Enjoy your meal.

Asian Pork Skewers

(Preparation time: 10 minutes | Cooking time: 15 minutes | Servings: 12)

Per serving: Calories 114, Total fat 3g, Protein 16g, Carbs 6g

Ingredients:

- 1 1/2 lbs. of pork tenderloin, cut into 1-inch pieces

For the marinade:

- 1/4 teaspoon of cayenne
- 1/2 cup of hoisin sauce
- 3/4 teaspoon of cornstarch
- 1/2 teaspoon of pepper
- 1 1/4 teaspoons of kosher salt
- 2 teaspoons of Five-spice powder

Instructions:

- Mix the pork chunks with the marinade ingredients in a mixing bowl & set aside for around 30 minutes to marinate.
- Preheat your griddle at medium-high.
- Coat the top of the griddle using cooking spray.
- Using skewers, thread marinated pork chunks.
- Cook the skewers for around 3-4 minutes on each side on a hot griddle.
- Enjoy your meal.

Pork Fillet with Fennel Seeds

(Preparation time: 15 minutes | Cooking time: 35 minutes | Servings: 4)

Per serving: Calories 204, Total fat 13g, Protein 32g, Carbs 2g

Ingredients:

- Olive oil to taste
- 21 oz. of pork tenderloin
- Salt & pepper to taste
- 3 tablespoons of fennel seeds

Instructions:

- Remove the excess fat out from the pork tenderloin by washing and drying it.
- Brush the fillet using olive oil, then season with salt, pepper, & fennel seeds all over.
- Tie the fillet using kitchen string to keep it from deforming during the cooking process.
- Preheat your griddle at 320°F and prepare your Blackstone for indirect cooking.
- Place the fillet on the griddle and cook for around 35 minutes, or till the internal temperature reaches 154°F.
- Remove the meat from the griddle after it has finished cooking and set it aside to rest for 10 minutes.
- Remove the kitchen thread after 10 minutes and slice them into slices.
- Serve the meat on serving platters.

Pork Loin Glazed with Honey

(Preparation time: 15 minutes | Cooking time: 60 minutes | Servings: 4)

Per serving: Calories 334, Total fat 10g, Protein 54g, Carbs 6g

Ingredients:

- 1/2 cup of honey
- 2 sprigs of thyme
- 35 oz. of pork loin
- Salt & pepper to taste
- 2 sprigs of rosemary
- Olive oil to taste
- 4 sage leaves
- ½ glass of meat broth

Instructions:

- In a mixing bowl, combine the honey, meat broth, 5 tablespoons olive oil, salt, & pepper till you get a uniform emulsion.

- Remove any excess fat out from the pork loin by washing and drying it.
- Place the meat in a bowl & pour the emulsion over it.
- Cover the bowl using cling film and marinate for 2 hours in the fridge.
- Preheat your griddle at 320°F and prepare your Blackstone for indirect cooking.
- Place them on the griddle and place the loin on it.
- Cook for 1 hour, or till the temperature of the meat reaches 167° F, with the probe in the center.
- Every 10 minutes, turn the meat and spray it using the marinade.
- Remove the meat from the griddle after it has finished cooking and set it aside to rest for 10 minutes.
- Cut the meat into pieces and arrange on serving dishes after 10 minutes.
- Serve with the marinade on the side.

Pork Rolls

(Preparation time: 15 minutes | Cooking time: 10 minutes | Servings: 4)

Per serving: Calories 405, Total fat 17g, Protein 55g, Carbs 2g

Ingredients:

- 3.5 oz. of sliced speck
- Salt & pepper to taste
- 8 slices of pork loin (3.5 oz. each)
- Olive oil to taste
- 3.5 oz. of sliced provolone

Instructions:

- Remove any excess fat out from the pork pieces by washing and drying them.
- Add a bit of salt and black pepper to taste.
- Inside each slice, add a slice of provolone & a slice of speck.
- Close the pork pieces by rolling them inwards and tying them together using kitchen thread.
- Preheat your griddle at 390°F and prepare your Blackstone for direct cooking.

- Place the meat on the griddle after brushing it with olive oil.
- Cook for around 10 minutes, flipping and spraying the rolls with olive oil as needed.
- Remove the rolls from the griddle and set them aside to cool for a few minutes.
- Remove the kitchen string and serve the rolls on their serving plates.

Pork Sausages in White Wine

(Preparation time: 10 minutes | Cooking time: 50 minutes | Servings: 4)

Per serving: Calories 809, Total fat 32g, Protein 31g, Carbs 10g

Ingredients:

- 2 glasses of white wine
- 8 pork sausages
- Olive oil to taste
- 2 cloves of garlic

Instructions:

- Preheat your Blackstone griddle at 280°F and prepare your Blackstone for indirect cooking.
- Once the griddle has reached the desired temperature, evenly space the sausages on the griddle.
- Cook for around 40 minutes, turning them over every 5 minutes with a little olive oil.
- Place the wine in a baking dish in the meantime.
- Garlic should be peeled and washed before being chopped and placed in the baking dish with wine.
- Remove the sausages from the griddle after 40 minutes and heat the wine.
- Place the sausages in the baking dish once the mixture begins to boil.
- Allow the sausages to rest for 15 minutes after turning off the griddle.
- Place the sausages on serving dishes after 15 minutes.
- Serve with a sprinkling of wine.

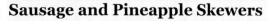

Sausage and Pineapple Skewers

(Preparation time: 15 minutes | Cooking time: 10 minutes | Servings: 4)

Per serving: Calories 357, Total fat 19g, Protein 15g, Carbs 9g

Ingredients:

- 2 tablespoons of mustard
- 14 oz. of sausage
- 1 teaspoon of chopped chives
- 14 oz. of pineapple pulp
- Salt & pepper to taste
- 2 tablespoons of balsamic vinegar
- Olive oil to taste
- 2 teaspoons of honey

Instructions:

- Wash & dry the pineapple before cutting it into pieces.
- Cut the sausage into the same size cubes as the pineapple.
- Alternately place meat cubes and pineapple cubes into the skewers to make the skewers.
- Prepare the marinating sauce in the meantime.
- Combine the mustard, vinegar, salt, honey, oil, chives, & pepper in a large-sized mixing dish.
- Place the skewers in the dish, cover them using plastic wrap, and marinate in the refrigerator for an hour.
- Preheat your Blackstone griddle at 390°F and prepare your Blackstone for direct cooking.
- Drain the skewers after marinating and set them immediately on the griddle.
- Cook for around 8 minutes, flipping the skewers on all sides.
- Remove them out from the griddle as soon as they're done, place them on plates, and serve right away.

Citrusy Butter Pork Chops

(Preparation time: 10 minutes | Cooking time: 30 minutes | Servings: 4)

Per serving: Calories 396, Total fat 17g, Protein 32g, Carbs 7g

Ingredients:

- 2 lemons, sliced into wedges
- 1 clove of garlic, minced
- 1 teaspoon of black pepper
- 2 oranges, sliced into wedges
- 6 sprigs of rosemary, chopped
- 5 pork chops
- 2 sticks of butter, softened
- 4 tablespoons of fresh thyme leave, chopped

Instructions:

- Preheat your Blackstone griddle at medium temperature and apply a thin layer of oil on the griddle.
- In a dish, squeeze the lemons and oranges. Except for the pork chops, combine the remaining ingredients in a mixing bowl.
- Marinate the pork chops for around 3 hours in the mixture. Cook for around 10 minutes per side on the griddle.

Simple and Easy Grilled Pork Tenderloin

(Preparation time: 10 minutes | Cooking time: 4 hours | Servings: 6)

Per serving: Calories 364, Total fat 22g, Protein 37g, Carbs 3g

Ingredients:

- 1 batch of Pork Rub
- 2 (around 1-pound/454 g) pork tenderloins

Instructions:

- Preheat your Blackstone griddle at 250°F and apply a thin layer of oil on the griddle.
- Season the tenderloins well using the rub. Work the rub into the meat using your hands.
- Put the tenderloins directly on the griddle and cook for around 4 to 5 hours, or till they reach 145°F (63°C) internal temperature.
- Remove the tenderloins out from the griddle & set them to rest for 5–10 minutes before slicing thinly & serving.

Garlic Spiced BBQ Tenderloin

(Preparation time: 10 minutes | Cooking time: 15 minutes | Servings: 4)

Per serving: Calories 183, Total fat 7g, Protein 27g, Carbs 2g

Ingredients:

- BBQ seasoning
- 1 pork tenderloin, silver skin removed & dried

For the fresh herb sauce:

- ¼ tablespoon of garlic powder
- ½ tablespoon of kosher salt
- 1 handful of basil, fresh
- ¼ cup of olive oil

Instructions:

- Preheat your Blackstone griddle at Medium temperature.
- Coat the pork in BBQ spice and roast it on the griddle over indirect heat. To achieve consistent cooking, turn the meat frequently.
- Cook till the internal temperature reaches 145°F. Remove the steak out from the griddle and set it aside to cool for around 10 minutes.
- Meanwhile, pounding all of the sauce ingredients into a food processor will make the herb sauce. Pulse a few times or till everything is well chopped.
- Serve the pork diagonally sliced with the sauce spooned on top. Serve & have fun.

Beef Recipes

- 2 teaspoons of olive oil, more for brushing
- Sea salt, to taste
- 2 tablespoons of balsamic vinegar
- 2 garlic cloves, minced
- Black pepper, to taste

Instructions:

- In a sealable plastic bag, combine marinade ingredients, add the steaks, seal bag, toss to coat, set it aside at room temperature for around 30 minutes.
- Preheat your Blackstone griddle at medium-high and apply a thin layer of oil on the griddle.
- Remove the steaks out from the marinade and set them on the griddle to cook for around 10 minutes per side. Place the steaks on a cutting board and set them aside to rest for 5 minutes.
- Slice the meat across the grain & serve with your favorite sides.

Grilled Tomahawk

(Preparation time: 20 minutes | Cooking time: 30 minutes | Servings: 4)

Per serving: Calories 540, Total fat 20g, Protein 66g, Carbs 2g

Ingredients:

- 2 bay leaves
- 4 juniper berries
- 42 oz. of Tomahawk
- Salt & pepper to taste
- 2 tablespoons of butter
- 1 sprig of rosemary
- Olive oil to taste
- 2 cloves of garlic
- 2 sage leaves

Instructions:

- Bay leaves, rosemary, & sage should be washed and dried.
- Garlic should be peeled and washed.
- In a blender glass, combine the butter, garlic, fragrant herbs & juniper berries, oil, salt, & pepper.

Flash-Marinated Skirt Steak

(Preparation time: 15 minutes | Cooking time: 25 minutes | Servings: 4)

Per serving: Calories 256, Total fat 14g, Protein 30g, Carbs 2g

Ingredients:

- 2 (8 ounces) of skirt steaks

For the marinade:

- Blend till the mixture is completely homogenous.
- Remove all extra fat from the meat after washing and drying it.
- On all sides, massage the meat using the flavored butter.
- Preheat your Blackstone griddle at 350°F and prepare your Blackstone for the direct cooking.
- Place the meat on the griddle & cook for around 10 minutes.
- Cook for another 5 minutes perpendicularly before turning it over.
- Carry out the same procedure on the other side.
- Remove the meat from the griddle and set it aside to rest for 10 minutes on a chopping board.
- Now chop the meat into slices & arrange them on serving dishes.

Grilled Rib-Eye Steak

(Preparation time: 15 minutes | Cooking time: 20 minutes | Servings: 4)

Per serving: Calories 420, Total fat 29g, Protein 60g, Carbs 2g

Ingredients:

- 4 sprigs of rosemary
- Salt & pepper to taste
- 4 ribs of beef (10 oz. each)
- Olive oil to taste
- 4 cloves of garlic

Instructions:

- Remove any excess fat from the beef ribs by washing and drying them.
- The rosemary should be washed and dried before being chopped finely.
- Garlic cloves should be peeled and washed before being chopped.
- In a mixing dish, combine the garlic, salt, pepper, & chopped rosemary.
- Preheat your Blackstone griddle at 350°F and prepare your Blackstone for the direct cooking.
- After brushing the ribs using olive oil, sprinkle a mixture of rosemary & garlic over the entire surface.

- Place the meat on the griddle, cover, and cook for around 15 minutes, or till the internal temperature has reached 131°F.
- Turn the meat after 3 minutes.
- Remove the meat out from the griddle after it has finished cooking and set it aside to rest for 5 minutes.
- Place the ribs on serving dishes & serve after 5 minutes.

Grilled Steaks with Potatoes

(Preparation time: 15 minutes | Cooking time: 20 minutes | Servings: 4)

Per serving: Calories 362, Total fat 13g, Protein 45g, Carbs 15g

Ingredients:

- 10.5 oz. of potatoes
- 4 beef steaks (7 oz. each)
- Salt & pepper to taste
- 2 sprigs of rosemary
- Olive oil to taste

Instructions:

- Let's begin with the potatoes. They should be peeled, washed, and then cut into wedges.
- Drain the potatoes after boiling them in salted water.
- Brush the potatoes using olive oil & place them in the baking pan.
- The rosemary should be washed and dried before being placed in the baking pan with potatoes.
- Preheat your Blackstone griddle at 390°F and prepare your Blackstone for the direct/indirect cooking.
- Cook for 15 minutes on indirect heat in the pan with the potatoes.
- Remove any excess fat from the steaks by washing and drying them.
- Season using salt & pepper after brushing them with the olive oil.
- Place the steaks on the direct heat.
- Cook for another 6 minutes before flipping the steaks.

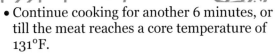

- Continue cooking for another 6 minutes, or till the meat reaches a core temperature of 131°F.
- Remove the meat & potatoes from the griddle once they've finished cooking.
- Place the steaks on the plates, top with the potatoes, & serve.

Grilled Beef Ribs

(Preparation time: 10 minutes | Cooking time: 20 minutes | Servings: 4)

Per serving: Calories 136, Total fat 13g, Protein 24g, Carbs 2g

Ingredients:

- 2 sprigs of rosemary
- Salt & pepper to taste
- 4 beef ribs (5 oz. each)
- Olive oil to taste
- 1 clove of garlic

Instructions:

- The rosemary should be cleaned and dried before being chopped.
- The garlic clove should be peeled & washed before being chopped.
- Remove any excess fat out from the beef ribs by washing and drying them.
- Season the ribs using oil, salt, rosemary, pepper, and garlic in a mixing bowl.
- Cover the bowl using cling film and refrigerate for 30 minutes to marinate.
- Remove the meat from the fridge after 30 minutes & set your Blackstone griddle for direct cooking at 390°F.
- Cook the ribs for 3 minutes on each side on the griddle.
- Remove the meat out from the griddle after it has finished cooking and set it aside to rest for 5 minutes.
- Place the ribs onto serving dishes and serve after 5 minutes.

Grapefruit Marinated Beef Ribs

(Preparation time: 10 minutes | Cooking time: 20 minutes | Servings: 4)

Per serving: Calories 552, Total fat 18g, Protein 52g, Carbs 6g

Ingredients:

- 8 mint leaves
- Olive oil to taste
- 4 beef cutlets (2 oz. each)
- 1 grapefruit
- 1 tablespoon of pink pepper
- Salt & pepper to taste.

Instructions:

- Squeeze the grapefruit juice into the bowl and drain it.
- Mint leaves should be washed and dried before being chopped.
- In a bowl with grapefruit juice, combine the mint, salt, pink pepper, 4 tablespoons of olive oil, and pepper.
- Mix till you get a homogenous emulsion.
- Remove any excess fat from the meat chops by washing and drying them.
- Place the ribs in the bowl with marinade, cover using plastic wrap, and set aside for 2 hours to marinate.
- Prepare your Blackstone griddle for direct cooking at 356°F at the end of the 2 hours.
- Place the ribs on the griddle and cook for around 8 minutes on each side, or till the meat reaches 140°F.
- Turn the meat a few times and spray it with the marinade often.
- Remove the ribs out from the griddle & set them aside for 10 minutes to rest in the marinade.
- Place the ribs on serving dishes and drizzle with a little marinade before serving.

Beefsteak in Red Wine

(Preparation time: 15 minutes | Cooking time: 15 minutes | Servings: 4)

Per serving: Calories 812, Total fat 25g, Protein 64g, Carbs 5g

Ingredients:

- 1 bottle of red wine
- Salt & pepper to taste
- 4 beef steaks (10.5 oz. each)
- 2 sprigs of rosemary
- Olive oil to taste

Instructions:

- To begin, wash the steak and blot it dry using a paper towel.
- Brush the steaks lightly using olive oil and season them with salt and black pepper.
- Rinse & dry the rosemary leaves.
- Now pour the red wine into a resalable bag.
- Close the bag and add the steaks and rosemary.
- Allow the steaks to marinate for at least 2 hours in the refrigerator.
- Remove the meat out from the fridge after two hours.
- Preheat your Blackstone griddle at 400°F and prepare your Blackstone griddle for the direct cooking.
- Remove the steaks from the red wine marinade.
- Cook the meat steaks over direct fire.
- Cook for around 10 minutes, or till the beef reaches a core temperature of 131° F, flipping occasionally.
- Remove the steaks out from the griddle and set them aside for around 10 minutes to rest.
- Remove the bone out from the steaks & chop them into strips before serving.
- Serve with a drizzle of oil, salt, and pepper.

Beef Sirloin with Aromatic Herbs

(Preparation time: 15 minutes | Cooking time: 20 minutes | Servings: 4)

Per serving: Calories 348, Total fat 16g, Protein 52g, Carbs 2g

Ingredients:

- 4 sprigs of rosemary
- 28 oz. of beef sirloin
- Olive oil to taste
- 4 sprigs of marjoram
- 4 sprigs of thyme
- Salt & pepper to taste
- 4 sage leaves

Instructions:

- Remove extra fat from the sirloin by washing and drying it.
- Thyme, marjoram, sage, and rosemary should be washed and dried before being chopped as fine as possible.
- In a bowl, combine the herbs, salt, pepper, & 4 tablespoons of olive oil.
- Brush the meat using the herb mixture after it has been thoroughly mixed.
- Preheat your Blackstone griddle at 400°F and prepare your Blackstone for the direct cooking.
- Place the meat on the griddle & cook for around 16 minutes, or till it reaches a temperature of 131°F.
- Brush the meat with the herb marinade regularly.
- Remove the meat out from the griddle after it has finished cooking and set it aside to rest for 10 minutes.
- Place the meat on a cutting board & slice it.
- Serve the meat on serving dishes, seasoned with a little herb marinade.

Aromatic Vinegar Beef Tenderloin

(Preparation time: 10 minutes | Cooking time: 20 minutes | Servings: 4)

Per serving: Calories 337, Total fat 10g, Protein 42g, Carbs 10g

Ingredients:

- Salt & pepper to taste
- 28 oz. of beef tenderloin
- Olive oil to taste
- 1 glass of balsamic vinegar

Instructions:

- Remove extra fat from the beef fillet by washing and drying it.
- Season the beef using oil, salt, pepper, & balsamic vinegar in a mixing bowl.
- Cover the bowl using cling film and refrigerate for around 2 hours to marinate.
- Remove the meat out from the fridge after the marinating time has passed.
- Preheat your Blackstone griddle at 390°F and prepare your Blackstone for the direct cooking.
- Cook the beef on the griddle for around 20 minutes, or till the internal temperature has reached 131°F.
- Brush the meat using the marinade on a regular basis.
- Remove the meat out from the griddle after it has finished cooking and set it aside to rest for 10 minutes.
- Cut the fillets into four slices after 10 minutes.
- Place the meat onto serving dishes and drizzle with the marinade before serving.

Carne Asada

(Preparation time: 10 minutes | Cooking time: 20 minutes | Servings: 4)

Per serving: Calories 363, Total fat 18g, Protein 42g, Carbs 8g

Ingredients:

- 1 orange, juiced
- 1 lb. of hanger steak or shirt steak
- 1/4 teaspoon of salt
- 1/4 cup of olive oil
- A handful of fresh cilantro, chopped
- 1 garlic clove, finely chopped
- 1/4 teaspoon of ground pepper
- 1 lime, juiced
- 1/2 teaspoon of cumin

Instructions:

- In a big sealable plastic bag, mix all of the ingredients. Refrigerate for around 1 to 2 hours to marinate.

- Preheat your Blackstone griddle at medium temperature and apply a thin layer of oil on the griddle.
- Cook for around 4 minutes on each side or till just cooked through.
- Allow resting for 10 minutes on a chopping board.
- Serve after slicing against the grain.

Coffee Crusted Skirt Steak

(Preparation time: 10 minutes | Cooking time: 20 minutes | Servings: 8)

Per serving: Calories 324, Total fat 16g, Protein 38g, Carbs 5g

Ingredients:

- 1/4 cup of dark brown sugar, firmly packed
- 1/8 teaspoon of ground cinnamon
- 2 1/2 lbs. of skirt steak, cut into 4 pieces
- 1/4 cup of coffee beans, finely ground
- 1 tablespoon of olive oil
- 1 1/2 teaspoon of sea salt
- Pinch of cayenne pepper

Instructions:

- Preheat your Blackstone griddle at medium-high temperature and apply a thin layer of oil on the griddle.
- To make the rub, combine coffee, cinnamon, brown sugar, salt, and cayenne pepper in a dish.
- Remove the steak out from the refrigerator and set aside for 15 minutes to come at room temperature. Oil the steak & season it using the spice rub. Rub the spice rub into the meat.
- Place on the griddle and cook for around 2 to 4 minutes on each side, sear till browned and medium-rare. Transfer it to a cutting board, wrap in foil, and set aside for 5 minutes before slicing thinly across the grain.

Flank Steak with Garlic and Rosemary

(Preparation time: 10 minutes | Cooking time: 20 minutes | Servings: 4)

Per serving: Calories 260, Total fat 13g, Protein 41g, Carbs 4g

Ingredients:

- 2 (8 ounces) of flank steaks

For the marinade:

- 4 cloves of garlic, minced
- 1 tablespoon of extra virgin olive oil, plus more for brushing
- 1/4 teaspoon of black pepper
- 2 tablespoons of fresh rosemary, chopped
- 2 teaspoons of sea salt

Instructions:

- Inside a food processor or blender, pulse the marinade ingredients till the garlic & rosemary are crushed.
- Prick the steaks Ten times on each side using a fork.
- On both sides, rub each using the marinade evenly.
- Refrigerate it for at least 1 hour or overnight in a covered dish.
- Preheat your Blackstone griddle at medium-high temperature and apply a thin layer of oil on the griddle.
- Cook for around 5 minutes on one side, then flip, tent using foil, & cook for another 3-4 minutes.
- Place the meat on a chopping board and cover using aluminum foil to rest for 15 minutes.
- Serve immediately after slicing very thinly against the grain.

Caprese Flank Steak

(Preparation time: 10 minutes | Cooking time: 15 minutes | Servings: 4)

Per serving: Calories 461, Total fat 23g, Protein 56g, Carbs 6g

Ingredients:

- 2 Roma tomatoes, sliced
- Sea salt for seasoning
- 4 (6 ounces) of flank steaks
- 8 fresh basil leaves
- Fresh ground pepper
- Balsamic vinegar glaze for drizzling
- Flakey sea salt, for serving
- Olive oil
- 4 ounces of fresh buffalo mozzarella, cut into four slices

Instructions:

- Brush each fillet using olive oil on all sides and sprinkle with salt & pepper.
- Preheat your Blackstone griddle at medium-high temperature and apply a thin layer of oil on the griddle. Place the steaks on the griddle and cook for around 5 minutes.
- Cook for an additional 5 minutes after flipping, re-tenting, and topping each with a piece of mozzarella during the last two minutes of cooking.
- Remove the steaks out from the griddle & serve with a few tomato slices and 2 basil leaves on top of each.
- Drizzle with the balsamic glaze and season with flaky salt and pepper to taste.

Teppanyaki Beef with Vegetables

(Preparation time: 10 minutes | Cooking time: 15 minutes | Servings: 6)

Per serving: Calories 484, Total fat 25g, Protein 51g, Carbs 14g

Ingredients:

Steak:

- 4 tablespoons of soy sauce
- 2 cups of snap peas
- 2- 1 lb. of sirloin steaks

- 3 tablespoons of butter
- 1 tablespoon of garlic powder
- 1 white onion, sliced into large rounds
- Salt & black pepper
- 3 zucchinis, sliced into ¼-inch thick flats
- 4 tablespoons of vegetable oil

Instructions:

- Salt, pepper, & garlic powder is used to season the steak.
- Set one side of your griddle at high and the other at medium temperature.
- Add the zucchini, onion rings, & snap peas to a medium-hot skillet with little vegetable oil on the griddle. Add a little of salt and pepper to taste.
- Cook the steaks for 3 minutes on the hot side. Flip the steaks, top with butter, and season using soy sauce. Continue to cook for another 4 minutes.
- Before serving, remove the steak and veggies from the griddle & slice the meat against the grain.

High-Low Strip Steak

(Preparation time: 10 minutes | Cooking time: 15 minutes | Servings: 6)

Per serving: Calories 347, Total fat 20g, Protein 39g, Carbs 4g

Ingredients:

- 2 (around 1-pound) New York strip steaks, trimmed

For the rub:

- 1 bunch of sage sprigs
- 1/2 teaspoon of garlic powder
- 1 bunch of thyme sprigs
- 2 tablespoons of extra-virgin olive oil
- 1 bunch of rosemary sprigs
- 1 1/2 teaspoons of black pepper, divided
- 2 tablespoons of chopped fresh flat-leaf parsley
- 3/4 teaspoon of sea salt, divided

Instructions:

- Preheat your Blackstone griddle at high and apply a thin layer of oil on the griddle.
- In a small-sized mixing dish, combine the rub ingredients and massage the steaks with the spice mixture; set aside for around 10 minutes.
- Cook the steaks for around 4 minutes on each side on the griddle.
- Reduce the temperature at medium on the griddle.
- Turn the steaks over and cook for another 3 minutes per side, or till the thermometer reads 135°F for the medium-rare.
- Place the steaks on a serving plate.
- Allow 5 minutes for resting. Thinly slice steaks across the grain.

Basic Juicy NY Strip Steak

(Preparation time: 20 minutes | Cooking time: 15 minutes | Servings: 2)

Per serving: Calories 560, Total fat 46g, Protein 84g, Carbs 2g

Ingredients:

- Sea salt
- 1 (8 ounces) of NY strip steak
- Fresh ground black pepper
- Olive oil

Instructions:

- Remove the steak out from the refrigerator & set it aside for around 30 to 45 minutes to come to room temperature.
- Brush the griddle using olive oil and preheat it at medium-high.
- Season the steak using salt and pepper on all sides.
- Cook the steak on the griddle for around 4 to 5 minutes on each side.
- Cook for another 4 minutes on the other side for a medium-rare steak that registers between 125°F & 130°F onto a meat thermometer.
- Before serving, transfer the steak to a platter and set aside for 5 minutes to rest.

Beef Pinwheels

(Preparation time: 10 minutes | Cooking time: 15 minutes | Servings: 4)

Per serving: Calories 363, Total fat 25g, Protein 30g, Carbs 2g

Ingredients:

- Olive oil for rubbing pinwheels
- 1 pound of Sirloin, cut into 4 1/2-inch thick pieces
- Freshly ground pepper
- 1 tablespoon of salt

For the stuffing:

- 2 tablespoons of pancetta
- 1 jar of red pesto
- 1 clove of garlic

Instructions:

- Preheat your Blackstone griddle at medium-high and apply a thin layer of oil on the griddle.
- Soak a dozen toothpicks in warm water before using.
- Inside a food processor or blender, add the filling ingredients and pulse till well incorporated.
- Pounded the sirloin pieces to a super-thin consistency.
- Season the sirloin chunks using oil, salt, & pepper to taste.
- Place a spoonful of filling on top of each piece.
- Roll up like a jelly roll & secure with moistened toothpicks on both ends.
- Cook the pinwheels for around 3 to 4 minutes on each side, flipping halfway through to ensure even cooking.
- Allow for a 5-minute pause before serving.

Lamb Recipes

- 1 teaspoon of red pepper flakes
- 1 tablespoon of lemon juice
- 1/4 cup of parsley
- Salt

Instructions:

- In a blender, combine all marinade ingredients & blend till smooth.
- Fill the mixing dish halfway with the combined mixture. Mix in the lamb chunks thoroughly and set aside for 2 hours to marinate.
- Using skewers, thread marinated lamb slices.
- Preheat your Blackstone griddle at medium-high.
- Coat the top of the griddle using cooking spray.
- Place the skewers on a heated griddle and cook for around 6 minutes, or till the lamb is done.
- Enjoy your meal.

Greek Lamb Patties

(Preparation time: 10 minutes | Cooking time: 15 minutes | Servings: 5)

Per serving: Calories 233, Total fat 8g, Protein 28g, Carbs 10g

Ingredients:

- 1 lb. of ground lamb
- 2 teaspoons of harissa paste
- 1 egg
- 1/4 cup of parsley, chopped
- 1/2 teaspoon of sumac
- 1 small onion, minced
- 1 1/2 teaspoons of ground coriander
- 1/2 cup of breadcrumbs
- 1 teaspoon of ground cumin
- 1 teaspoon of garlic, minced
- Salt & pepper to taste

Instructions:

- In a mixing bowl, combine all of the ingredients & stir till well blended.
- Preheat your Blackstone griddle at medium-high.
- Coat the top of the griddle using cooking spray.

Lamb Skewers

(Preparation time: 10 minutes | Cooking time: 15 minutes | Servings: 4)

Per serving: Calories 656, Total fat 51g, Protein 49g, Carbs 3g

Ingredients:

- 1 1/2 lbs. leg of lamb, cut into 1-inch pieces

For the marinade:

- 3/4 cup of olive oil
- 1 tablespoon of vinegar
- 1 teaspoon of ground cumin
- 1/4 cup of chives
- 1 1/2 teaspoon of paprika
- 1/4 cup of mint
- 2 tablespoons of shallot

- Make patties using the ingredients and cook for around 5 minutes on each side on a hot griddle.
- Enjoy your meal.

Tandoori lamb chops

(Preparation time: 15 minutes | Cooking time: 20 minutes | Servings: 4)

Per serving: Calories 331, Total fat 13g, Protein 40g, Carbs 2g

Ingredients:

- 1 tablespoon of tandoori spices
- 28 oz. of lamb chops
- Salt & pepper to taste
- 2 cloves of garlic
- Olive oil to taste

Instructions:

- Garlic cloves should be peeled and washed before being chopped.
- Remove extra excess fat from the lamb chops by washing and drying them.
- In a baking dish, place the ribs. Season them using oil, salt, and pepper before sprinkling spices and garlic on top.
- Cover the baking dish using cling film and marinate for 1 hour in the refrigerator.
- Remove the meat out from the fridge after an hour.
- Preheat your Blackstone griddle at 390°F and prepare your Blackstone for the direct cooking.
- Cook the chops on the griddle for around 5 minutes on each side.
- Remember to spray the meat using the marinade on a regular basis.
- Remove the meat out from the griddle after it has finished cooking and set it aside to rest for 5 minutes.
- Place the chops onto serving dishes and sprinkle with olive oil before serving.

Lamb Souvlaki

(Preparation time: 15 minutes | Cooking time: 15 minutes | Servings: 4)

Per serving: Calories 310, Total fat 14g, Protein 46g, Carbs 2g

Ingredients:

- 2 lemons
- 28 oz. of lamb loin
- Salt & pepper to taste
- 3.5 oz. of bacon
- 1 teaspoon of dried oregano
- Olive oil as needed

Instructions:

- Remove any excess fat from the lamb loin after washing and drying it.
- Put it in a dish and cut it into cubes.
- Oil, salt, pepper, dried oregano, & strained lemon juice are used to season the meat.
- Cover the bowl using cling film and place it in the refrigerator for 6 hours to marinate.
- Remove the meat out from the fridge and assemble the skewers after 6 hours.
- Make cubes out of the bacon. Place a cube of beef on the skewer, followed by a cube of bacon.
- Continue in this manner till all the ingredients have been used.
- Preheat your Blackstone griddle at 400°F and prepare your Blackstone for the direct cooking.
- Cook the skewers for around 3 minutes on each side on the griddle, coating with the marinade often.
- After the skewers have finished cooking, take them from the griddle and set them straight on the serving plates.

Danish Blue Lamb Chops

(Preparation time: 15 minutes | Cooking time: 15 minutes | Servings: 4)

Per serving: Calories 614, Total fat 31g, Protein 52g, Carbs 2g

Ingredients:

- ½ cup of crumbled Danish blue cheese
- 8 (around 3 ounces) lamb chops

- Ground black pepper to taste
- 2 tablespoons of heavy whipping cream
- 1 clove of garlic

Instructions:

- Preheat your Blackstone griddle at 350°F and apply a thin layer of oil on the griddle.
- Each lamb chop should be coated using garlic cloves on both sides and seasoned using black pepper.
- To make a paste, put blue cheese and cream in a mixing bowl.
- Cook lamb chops for around 5 to 6 minutes on each side on the griddle, or till no longer pinkish in the center. An instant-read thermometer placed into the center should read 145°F.
- Spread the cheese paste evenly on one side of each chop.
- Continue to cook for another 1 to 2 minutes, or till the cheese is browned & bubbling.

Tandoori Skewers

(Preparation time: 15 minutes | Cooking time: 15 minutes | Servings: 10)

Per serving: Calories 194, Total fat 12g, Protein 15g, Carbs 9g

Ingredients:

- 1 cup of plain yogurt
- ½ cup of lemon juice
- 2 pounds of boneless lamb shoulder, cut into small chunks
- 1 tablespoon of olive oil
- 1/2 cup of Tandoori masala

Instructions:

- Combine all of the ingredients in a mixing bowl, except for the lamb, in a mixing bowl.
- Toss the lamb into the marinade, making sure that all of the pieces are evenly coated. After putting the mixture in plastic wrap, refrigerate it overnight or for at least 4 hours.
- Skewer the lamb chunks together with skewers so that they barely touch. Wipe away any excess marinade using a paper towel. After brushing with vegetable oil, sprinkle with salt.
- Preheat your Blackstone griddle at 350°F and apply a thin layer of oil on the griddle.
- Cook the skewers for around 5 to 8 minutes on each side, or till the lamb returns to its original shape.
- Garnish with red onions, lemon wedges, & chopped cilantro, if preferred.

Garlic and Herb Lamb

(Preparation time: 10 minutes | Cooking time: 2 hours | Servings: 10)

Per serving: Calories 235, Total fat 14g, Protein 25g, Carbs 2g

Ingredients:

- 3 cloves of garlic, cut into slivers
- 1 teaspoon of dried rosemary, crushed
- 1 leg of lamb (around 5 pounds)
- 3 teaspoons of dried dill weed
- 1 ½ teaspoon of salt and black pepper

Instructions:

- Preheat your Blackstone griddle at 350°F.
- Use the tip of a knife to pierce the leg of the lamb far enough to allow garlic slivers to slide through. Dill, salt, & rosemary are rubbed into the leg of lamb. Place the lamb fat side up on a rack in a shallow grill pan.
- Roast for around 2 to 2 1/2 hours, or till an internal temp of 155°F is reached for medium. Tent using aluminum foil and put aside for 15 to 20 minutes before cutting. The lamb will continue to simmer for a few minutes more, thickening the juices and making carving simpler.

Rosemary-Thyme Lamb Chops

(Preparation time: 10 minutes | Cooking time: 30 minutes | Servings: 4)

Per serving: Calories 231, Total fat 9g, Protein 32g, Carbs 3g

Ingredients:

- 3 tablespoons of Dijon mustard
- 1 tablespoon of minced fresh thyme
- 8 lamb loin chops (around 3 ounces each)
- 3 minced garlic cloves
- 1 tablespoon of minced fresh rosemary

Instructions:

- Using a bit of salt and pepper, season your lamb chops. In a small-sized bowl, combine the mustard, rosemary, thyme, & garlic.
- Preheat your Blackstone griddle at 350°F and apply a thin layer of oil on top of the griddle.
- On an oiled griddle, cook for around 10 minutes. Brush the herb mixture over the chops on the other side. Cook for around 6-8 minutes more, or till the meat reaches the desired doneness (a thermometer should read 135°F for medium-rare, 140° for medium, & 145° for medium-well).

Skewered Lamb with Blackberry-Balsamic Glaze

(Preparation time: 10 minutes | Cooking time: 20 minutes | Servings: 4)

Per serving: Calories 255, Total fat 9g, Protein 32g, Carbs 9g

Ingredients:

- 1/3 cup of balsamic vinegar
- 1 tablespoon of Dijon mustard
- 1/2 cup of seedless blackberry spreadable fruit
- 1-1/2 pounds of lean boneless lamb, cut into 1-inch cubes
- 1 tablespoon of minced fresh rosemary

Instructions:

- In a small-sized mixing bowl, combine the rosemary, spreadable fruit, vinegar, & mustard. Pour 2/3 cup of the marinade onto a shallow dish and add the lamb after turning to coat, cover & chill for at least 1 hour. Cover and refrigerate the remaining marinade for basting.

- Remove the lamb out from the dish and discard the marinade. 6 skewers, strung with lamb, metal or moistened wooden.
- Preheat your Blackstone griddle at 350° and apply a thin layer of oil on the griddle.
- On a griddle, arrange the kabobs. Cook for around 10-12 minutes, flipping once or twice and basting with the leftover marinade till the lamb is done to your liking (a thermometer should read 135°F for medium-rare, 140°F for medium, and 145°F for medium-well).

Spicy Chinese Cumin Lamb Skewers

(Preparation time: 10 minutes | Cooking time: 15 minutes | Servings: 10)

Per serving: Calories 77, Total fat 5g, Protein 6g, Carbs 2g

Ingredients:

- 2 tablespoons of ground cumin
- 1 pound of lamb shoulder, cut into 1/2-inch pieces
- 1 tablespoon of salt
- 10 skewers
- 2 tablespoons of red pepper flakes

Instructions:

- Thread a part of the lamb chunks onto a flat kebab skewer. Continue with the remaining meat and skewers.
- Preheat your Blackstone griddle at 350°F and apply a thin layer of oil on the griddle.
- On the griddle, skewers should be positioned. Cook for around 6 minutes, turning regularly & seasoning with the red pepper flakes, cumin, and salt till the meat is beautifully browned and no longer pink in the center.

Lamb Chops in Duck Sauce

(Preparation time: 20 minutes | Cooking time: 1 hour 20 minutes | Servings: 6)

Per serving: Calories 819, Total fat 61g, Protein 37g, Carbs 25g

Ingredients:

- 2 tablespoons of Worcestershire sauce
- Cayenne pepper to taste
- 3 pounds of lamb chops
- 1 ½ cups of duck sauce
- 1 tablespoon of adobo seasoning

Instructions:

- Coat the lamb chops evenly with adobo seasoning, Worcestershire sauce, & cayenne pepper in a medium baking dish.
- Preheat your Blackstone griddle at 200°F and apply a thin layer of oil on the griddle. Cook for approximately 1 hour on the griddle.
- Cook for another 15 to 20 minutes, or till the internal temperature of the lamb chops reaches 145°F.

Marinated Balsamic Lamb Chops

(Preparation time: 10 minutes | Cooking time: 20 minutes | Servings: 2)

Per serving: Calories 315, Total fat 26g, Protein 15g, Carbs 4g

Ingredients:

- 2 tablespoons of olive oil
- 2 tablespoons of chopped fresh mint plus 3 mint leaves
- 2 tablespoons of balsamic vinegar
- 2 lamb shoulder blade chops
- 2 tablespoons of soy sauce

Instructions:

- Preheat your Blackstone griddle at 450°F and apply a thin layer of oil on the griddle.
- Keep the marinade in the dish while cooking the lamb chops. Cook lamb chops for around 5 minutes on each side, rotating once, till the center is just pink. An instant-read thermometer placed in the center should read at least 145°F. To serve, arrange on a dish.
- Bring a small pot halfway full of the reserved marinade to the boil on the griddle. Cook for about 10 minutes, or till the marinade has been reduced to half its original volume. Serve with

the mint leaves as a garnish over the lamb chops.

Crispy and Spicy Lamb Chops

(Preparation time: 10 minutes | Cooking time: 15 minutes | Servings: 6)

Per serving: Calories 577, Total fat 16g, Protein 19g, Carbs 2g

Ingredients:

- 1 tablespoon of minced garlic
- ¼ cup of the white vinegar
- 2 tablespoons of olive oil
- ½ tablespoon of black pepper
- 2 lbs. of lamb chops (around 90 g)
- 1 thinly sliced onion
- 2 tablespoons of salt

Instructions:

- In a resealable bag, combine the vinegar, salt, sliced onion, black pepper, garlic, & oil till the salt is completely dissolved.
- Toss the lamb chunks in the sauce till well coated. Refrigerate for at least 2 hours to marinate.
- Preheat your Blackstone griddle at 450°F and apply a thin layer of oil.
- Remove the lamb out from the fridge and discard the marinade. The foil should be wrapped around any exposed bones.
- On the griddle, cook the lamb for around 5 minutes on each side. Cook in a broiler for extra crispiness. Serve & have a good time!

Tarragon Spiced Grilled Lamb

(Preparation time: 10 minutes | Cooking time: 15 minutes | Servings: 4)

Per serving: Calories 287, Total fat 12g, Protein 33g, Carbs 11g

Ingredients:

- 2 tablespoons of ground ginger
- 1 tablespoon of ground cinnamon
- 4 lamb chops
- ¼ cup of brown sugar
- 1 tablespoon of garlic powder
- 2 tablespoon tarragon, dried
- ½ tablespoon of salt
- 1 tablespoon of ground black pepper

Instructions:

- In a mixing bowl, combine the sugar, ginger, dried tarragon, garlic, cinnamon, black pepper, & salt.
- Season the lamb chops using salt and pepper to taste and arrange on a plate.
- Allow for a one-hour chilling period to allow the flavors to mingle.
- Preheat your Blackstone griddle at 400°F.
- Cook the lamb chops on the griddle in a single layer for around 5 minutes on each side.
- Serve and have a good time!

Fish and Seafood Recipes

- Tuna fillets should be washed and dried.
- After thoroughly mixing, dip the tuna into the marinade.
- Refrigerate for around 30 minutes after covering the bowl using cling film.
- Remove the tuna out from the fridge after marinating and prepare the Blackstone for the direct cooking at 390°F.
- Place the tuna fillet on the griddle and cook for around 6 minutes, flipping it frequently and coating it with the marinade continuously.
- Remove the tuna out from the griddle and set it on a chopping board once it has finished cooking.
- Place the tuna slices on serving plates cut them into small slices.
- Serve with a drizzle of the marinade.

Tuna Glazed with Soy Sauce

(Preparation time: 15 minutes | Cooking time: 30 minutes| Servings: 4)

Per serving: Calories 280, Total fat 12g, Protein 27g, Carbs 4g

Ingredients:

- 4 tablespoons of soy sauce
- 1 tablespoon of sesame seeds
- 21 oz. of tuna fillet
- 4 basil leaves
- Olive oil as needed
- ½ glass of balsamic vinegar
- Pepper to taste

Instructions:

- In a mixing bowl, combine the soy sauce, 4 tablespoons of olive oil, pepper, sesame seeds, & balsamic vinegar.

Hot and Spicy Torgrashi Salmon

(Preparation time: 10 minutes | Cooking time: 20 minutes| Servings: 3)

Per serving: Calories 250, Total fat 6g, Protein 11g, Carbs 4g

Ingredients:

- ¼ cup of olive oil
- 1 tablespoon of Togarashi seasoning
- 1 salmon fillet
- ½ tablespoon kosher salt
- ½ tablespoon of black pepper

Instructions:

- Preheat your Blackstone griddle at 400°F.
- Place the salmon skin-side down on a nonstick foil-lined baking sheet.
- Season the meat using black pepper, salt, & Togarashi after rubbing it with the oil.
- Cook the salmon on the griddle for around 20 minutes, or till the internal temperature reaches 145°F.
- Remove it from the griddle & serve right away.

Tuna with Sesame

(Preparation time: 15 minutes | Cooking time: 15 minutes| Servings: 4)

Per serving: Calories 197, Total fat 10g, Protein 12g, Carbs 2g

Ingredients:

- 1 tablespoon of white sesame seeds
- Salt & pepper to taste
- 21 oz. of tuna fillet
- 1 tablespoon of black sesame seeds
- Olive oil as needed
- 1 lemon

Instructions:

- The tuna fillet should be washed and dried.
- Season the tuna using filtered lemon juice, oil, salt, & pepper in a mixing bowl.
- Allow 15 minutes for the tuna to rest.
- Place the sesame seeds on a plate and then slide the tuna fillet over it several times to coat the entire surface.
- Preheat your Blackstone griddle at 390°F and prepare your Blackstone for the direct cooking.
- Allow 10 minutes for the cast-iron plate to heat up on the griddle.
- Place the tuna on the plate & cook for around 8 minutes, flipping it over halfway through.
- Remove the tuna out from the griddle and set it on a chopping board once it has finished cooking.
- Slice the tuna and arrange it on serving dishes.
- Serve with a small amount of marinade.

Lobster Tails with Citrus Butter

(Preparation time: 10 minutes | Cooking time: 40 minutes| Servings: 4)

Per serving: Calories 210, Total fat 20g, Protein 21g, Carbs 9g

Ingredients:

- 2 minced garlic cloves
- Salt & freshly ground black pepper, to taste
- ½ cup of butter, melted
- 4 lobster tails
- 2 teaspoons of fresh lemon juice

Instructions:

- Preheat your Blackstone griddle at 400°F.
- In a metal pan, combine all ingredients, except for the lobster tails, and stir well.
- Using the pan, cook for around 10 minutes on the griddle.
- Remove the top of the lobster shell to uncover the meat in the meantime.
- Take the butter mixture out of the griddle and set it aside.
- Apply a thin layer of oil on top of the griddle.
- Coat the lobster meat in the butter mixture.
- Cook the lobster tails for around 15 minutes on the griddle, basting halfway through using the butter mixture.
- Take them off the griddle and serve right away.

Tuna with Pistachio Sauce

(Preparation time: 15 minutes | Cooking time: 10 minutes| Servings: 4)

Per serving: Calories 307, Total fat 12g, Protein 31g, Carbs 5g

Ingredients:

- 4 parsley leaves
- 21 oz. of tuna fillet
- Salt & pepper to taste
- 2 tablespoons of chopped pistachios
- ½ lemon
- Olive oil as needed
- 1 sprig of rosemary

Instructions:

- Put the tuna fillet in a dish after washing and drying it.
- The rosemary should be washed and dried.
- In the same bowl as the tuna, combine the rosemary, filtered lemon juice, oil, salt, & pepper.
- Cover the bowl & marinate for around 30 minutes in the fridge.
- Wash & dry the parsley in the meantime.

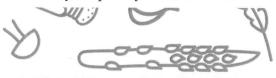

- In the mixer's glass, combine the salt, chopped pistachios, parsley, oil, and pepper.
- Blend with the mixer till the sauce is smooth and homogeneous.
- Remove the tuna out from the fridge after 30 minutes.
- Preheat your Blackstone griddle at 350°F and prepare your Blackstone for the direct cooking.
- Cook the tuna for around 3 minutes on each side on the griddle.
- Remove the tuna out from the griddle after it has finished cooking, place it on a cutting board, and cut it into slices.
- Place the tuna pieces on plates to serve.
- Serve with a dollop of pistachio sauce over the top.

Citrusy Scallops

(Preparation time: 10 minutes | Cooking time: 15 minutes| Servings: 4)

Per serving: Calories 100, Total fat 2g, Protein 17g, Carbs 3g

Ingredients:

- 2 tablespoons of kosher salt
- Squeeze lemon juice
- 2 lbs. (907 g) of sea scallops, dried with a paper towel
- 4 tablespoons of salted butter
- ½ tablespoon of garlic salt

Instructions:

- Preheat your Blackstone griddle at 400°F.
- Season the scallops on both sides using salt & black pepper.
- After the butter has been added, place the scallops on the cast iron and cook for around 8 minutes.
- After flipping the scallops, replace the lid. Cook for a further 8 minutes.
- Remove the scallops from the griddle and drizzle using lemon juice. Serve immediately & enjoy!

Tuna with Citrus Fruits

(Preparation time: 10 minutes | Cooking time: 10 minutes| Servings: 4)

Per serving: Calories 362, Total fat 16g, Protein 58g, Carbs 4g

Ingredients:

- 20 black olives
- Olive oil to taste
- 28 oz. of tuna fillet
- 1 orange
- Salt & pepper to taste
- 1 lemon
- 1 sprig of chopped parsley

Instructions:

- Put the tuna fillet in a dish after washing and drying it.
- The lemon & orange should be washed and dried. Grate the citrus zest & strain the juice into the tuna bowl.
- Add the oil, salt, & pepper, cover the bowl, and marinate for around 30 minutes in the refrigerator.
- Remove the tuna out from the fridge after marinating.
- Preheat your Blackstone griddle at 350°F and prepare your Blackstone for the direct cooking.
- Place the plate on the griddle for around 10 minutes to heat up.
- Brush the tuna fillet & black olives on top of the tuna marinade-coated platter.
- Remove the tuna & olives from the platter after 8 minutes of cooking, continue brushing with marinade.
- Place the tuna on a cutting board & slice it.
- Place the tuna slices and olives on the serving platters.
- Season with a dash of the marinade and a sprinkling of minced parsley before serving.

Easy Lobster Tail

(Preparation time: 10 minutes | Cooking time: 15 minutes| Servings: 2)

Per serving: Calories 91, Total fat 2g, Protein 2g, Carbs 1g

Ingredients:

- ¼ tablespoon of old bay seasoning
- 2 tablespoons of melted butter
- Cayenne pepper as required
- Oregano as required
- 10 oz. (283 g) of lobster tail
- 1 tablespoon of chopped fresh parsley
- ¼ tablespoon of Himalayan sea salt

Instructions:

- Preheat your Blackstone griddle at 400°F and apply a thin layer of oil on the top of griddle.
- Cut the tails down the middle using a knife.
- Before laying the tails on the griddle, season them using salt, cayenne pepper, oregano, & black pepper.
- Cook for around 15 minutes, or till an internal temperature of 140°F.
- Remove the tails, butter them, and sprinkle them using parsley.
- Serve & have a good time.

Yummy Barbecued Shrimp

(Preparation time: 10 minutes | Cooking time: 15 minutes| Servings: 4)

Per serving: Calories 227, Total fat 5g, Protein 37g, Carbs 7g

Ingredients:

- 1 pound (454 g) of peeled & deveined shrimp, with tails on
- Salt as needed
- 2 tablespoons of olive oil
- Black pepper as needed
- 1 batch of Dill Seafood Rub

Instructions:

- Soak wooden skewers in water for around 30 minutes.

- Preheat your Blackstone griddle at 375°F and apply a thin layer of oil on top of the griddle.
- Thread around 4 or 5 shrimp onto each skewer.
- Season the skewers on the both sides with a rub, then coat the shrimp with olive oil, salt, & black pepper.
- Cook your shrimp on skewers on the griddle for around 5 minutes on each side. Remove the skewers out from the griddle and serve immediately.

Honey-Lime Tilapia and Corn Foil Pack

(Preparation time: 10 minutes | Cooking time: 15 minutes | Servings: 4)

Per serving: Calories 319, Total fat 15g, Protein 24g, Carbs 20g

Ingredients:

- 4 limes, thinly sliced
- 1/4 cup of olive oil
- 4 fillets tilapia
- 2 tablespoons of fresh cilantro leaves
- Freshly ground black pepper
- 2 tablespoons of honey
- 2 ears corn, shucked
- Kosher salt

Instructions:

- Preheat your Blackstone griddle at high temperature and apply a thin layer of oil on top of the griddle.
- Cut 4 foil squares about 12" long.
- Place a piece of tilapia on top of each piece of foil.
- Tilapia should be brushed using honey & topped with lime, corn, and cilantro.
- Season using sea salt and black pepper and drizzle little olive oil.
- Cook for around 15 minutes on the griddle, or till the tilapia is cooked through and the corn is soft.

Halibut Fillets with Spinach and Olives

(Preparation time: 10 minutes | Cooking time: 15 minutes | Servings: 4)

Per serving: Calories 773, Total fat 37g, Protein 109g, Carbs 4g

Ingredients:

- 4 cups of baby spinach
- 2 tablespoons of flat-leaf parsley, chopped
- 4 (6 ounces) of halibut fillets
- Lemon wedges, to Servings
- 1/3 cup of olive oil
- 1/4 cup of lemon juice
- 2 teaspoons of fresh dill, chopped
- 2 ounces of pitted black olives, halved

Instructions:

- Preheat your Blackstone griddle at medium-high heat and apply a thin layer of oil on top of the griddle.
- In a mixing dish, toss the spinach with the lemon juice & leave it aside.
- Cook on the griddle for around 3-4 minutes on each side, or till fish is cooked through, brushing with the olive oil.
- Remove from the griddle, cover, & set aside for 5 minutes.
- Cook for around 2 minutes, or till spinach is slightly wilted, with the remaining oil. Remove it from the griddle.
- Transfer to serving plates containing the fish and lemon wedges after tossing with olives and herbs.

Gremolata Swordfish Skewers

(Preparation time: 15 minutes | Cooking time: 15 minutes | Servings: 4)

Per serving: Calories 333, Total fat 16g, Protein 44g, Carbs 3g

Ingredients:

- 3 tablespoons of lemon juice
- 2 teaspoons of garlic, minced
- 1 1/2 lbs. of skinless swordfish fillet
- 2 tablespoons of extra-virgin olive oil, plus extra for serving
- 3 lemons, cut into slices
- 2 teaspoons of lemon zest
- 1/2 cup of finely chopped parsley
- 1/4 teaspoon of black pepper
- 1/2 teaspoon of red pepper flakes
- 3/4 teaspoon of sea salt

Instructions:

- Preheat your Blackstone griddle at medium-high temperature and apply a thin layer of oil on top of the griddle.
- Set aside gremolata, which is made by combining lemon zest, parsley, garlic, 1/4 teaspoon salt, & pepper in a small-sized bowl using a fork.
- Combine swordfish chunks, lemon juice, red pepper flakes, olive oil, and the remaining salt
- Alternate threading swordfish & lemon slices onto metal skewers.
- Cook skewers for around 8 to 10 minutes on the griddle, or till fish is cooked through, flipping halfway through.
- Serve the skewers with gremolata on a serving plate.
- Serve with a drizzle of olive oil.

Spiced Crab Legs

(Preparation time: 5 minutes | Cooking time: 10 minutes | Servings: 2)

Per serving: Calories 518, Total fat 14g, Protein 87g, Carbs 3g

Ingredients:

- 2 tablespoons of chili oil
- 4 lbs. of king crab legs, cooked

Instructions:

- Preheat your Blackstone griddle at high temperature and apply a thin layer of oil on top of the griddle.

- Place crab legs on griddle and brush both sides using chili oil. Make a foil tent.
- Cook for around 4 to 5 minutes on each side, flipping once.
- Using pulled butter, transfer to plates & serve.

Lump Crab Cakes

(Preparation time: 10 minutes | Cooking time: 15 minutes | Servings: 4)

Per serving: Calories 282, Total fat 27g, Protein 19g, Carbs 9g

Ingredients:

- 1/2 cup of panko breadcrumbs
- 2 teaspoons of Worcestershire sauce
- 1 egg, beaten
- 1/2 teaspoon of salt
- 1 lb. of lump crab meat
- 3 tablespoons of vegetable oil
- 1/3 cup of mayonnaise
- 2 tablespoons of Dijon mustard
- 1/2 teaspoon of paprika
- 1/4 teaspoon of black pepper

Instructions:

- Preheat your Blackstone griddle at medium-high temperature and apply a thin layer of oil on top of the griddle.
- In a large-sized bowl, combine the crab, breadcrumbs, mayo, salt, egg, mustard Worcestershire sauce, paprika, & pepper. To blend, whisk everything together thoroughly.
- Shape the crab mixture into four large balls and slightly flatten them.
- Cook the crab cakes for approximately 5 minutes on each side on the griddle, or till golden & crispy. Serves right away.
-
-

Spicy Grilled Jumbo Shrimp

(Preparation time: 10 minutes | Cooking time: 15 minutes | Servings: 6)

Per serving: Calories 131, Total fat 8g, Protein 14g, Carbs 2g

Ingredients:

- 1-1/2 pounds of uncooked jumbo shrimp, peeled & deveined

For the marinade:

- 1 teaspoon of chili powder
- 1/4 cup of olive oil
- 2 tablespoons of fresh parsley
- 1/8 teaspoon of pepper
- 1 bay leaf, dried
- 1 teaspoon of garlic powder
- 1/4 teaspoon of salt
- 1/4 teaspoon of cayenne pepper

Instructions:

- In a food processor, combine the marinade ingredients and pulse till smooth.
- In a large-sized mixing bowl, pour the marinade.
- Refrigerate, covered, for around 30 minutes after adding the shrimp and tossing to coat.
- Using metal skewers, thread shrimp onto them.
- Preheat your Blackstone griddle at medium-high temperature and apply a thin layer of oil on top of the griddle.
- Cook on the griddle, flipping once, for around 5-6 minutes, or till shrimp are opaque pink.
- Serves right away.

Coconut Pineapple Shrimp Skewers

(Preparation time: 20 minutes | Cooking time: 15 minutes | Servings: 4)

Per serving: Calories 150, Total fat 11g, Protein 2g, Carbs 15g

Ingredients:

- 1 tablespoon of cilantro, chopped
- 1-1/2 pounds of uncooked jumbo shrimp, peeled and deveined
- 1/4 cup of freshly squeezed orange juice

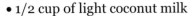

- 1/2 cup of light coconut milk
- 1/4 cup of freshly squeezed lime juice (from about 2 large limes)
- 4 teaspoons of Tabasco Original Red Sauce
- Olive oil for grilling
- 2 teaspoons of soy sauce
- 3/4 pound of pineapple, cut into 1-inch chunks

Instructions:

- Mix together the coconut milk, cilantro, orange juice, Tabasco sauce, soy sauce, & lime juice in a mixing bowl. Toss in the shrimp to coat them.
- Cover and marinate for one hour in the refrigerator.
- Alternate threading shrimp & pineapple onto metal skewers.
- Preheat your Blackstone griddle at medium-high temperature and apply a thin layer of oil on top of the griddle.
- Cook, flipping once, for around 5-6 minutes, or till shrimp are opaque pink.
- Serve right away.

Mexican Shrimp Tacos

(Preparation time: 10 minutes | Cooking time: 10 minutes | Servings: 4)

Per serving: Calories 400, Total fat 15g, Protein 24g, Carbs 30g

Ingredients:

- 1 bag of cabbage slaw
- 2 lbs. of medium shrimp, peeled and deveined
- 1 cup of Mexican crema
- 8 flour tortillas, warmed
- 1 cup of salsa

For the marinade:

- 1 tablespoon of cumin
- 1 tablespoon of fresh lime juice
- 2 tablespoons of olive oil
- ⅛ teaspoon of fresh ground pepper
- 1 tablespoon of chili powder
- 1 tablespoon of garlic powder
- ¼ teaspoon of sea salt

Instructions:

- Preheat your Blackstone griddle at medium-high temperature and apply a thin layer of oil on top of it.
- In a big sealable plastic bag, combine the oil marinade ingredients. Toss in the shrimp & marinate for around 30 minutes in the refrigerator.
- Cook for around 5 minutes on each side, or till shrimp are cooked through.
- Place on a plate to cool.
- On each plate, place two tortillas. In the center of each tortilla, evenly distribute the shrimp, cabbage slaw, & salsa.
- Serve with Mexican crema drizzled on top.

Scallops with Lemony Salsa Verde

(Preparation time: 10 minutes | Cooking time: 10 minutes | Servings: 2)

Per serving: Calories 267, Total fat 10g, Protein 32g, Carbs 14g

Ingredients:

- 12 large sea scallops, side muscle removed
- Sea salt for seasoning
- 1 tablespoon of olive oil, plus more for grilling

For the Lemony Salsa Verde:

- 1 small shallot, finely chopped
- ¼ cup of chopped fresh chives
- ¾ cup of finely chopped fresh parsley
- ½ lemon, with peel, seeded & chopped
- 5 tomatillos, peeled & pulsed in a blender
- ¼ teaspoon of black pepper
- 1 garlic clove, finely chopped
- ½ cup of finely chopped fresh cilantro
- ¼ cup of olive oil
- ¼ teaspoon of sea salt

Instructions:

- Set aside the ingredients for the Lemony Salsa in a small-sized mixing dish.
- Brush the griddle using olive oil and preheat it at medium-high temperature.
- On a baking pan, toss scallops using 1 tablespoon of olive oil and season with the salt.

- Add scallops to griddle and cook for around 45 seconds to 1 minute, rotating once. Before removing from the griddle, cook for an extra minute.
- Serve the scallops with a lemony salsa verde on top.

Oysters with Spiced Tequila Butter

(Preparation time: 10 minutes | Cooking time: 25 minutes | Servings: 6)

Per serving: Calories 184, Total fat 15g, Protein 2g, Carbs 4g

Ingredients:

- Flakey sea salt, for serving
- 3 dozen medium oysters, scrubbed & shucked

For the butter:

- 7 tablespoons of unsalted butter
- 2 tablespoons of freshly squeezed lemon juice
- 1/4 teaspoon of crushed red pepper
- 1 teaspoon of dried oregano
- 2 tablespoons of tequila Blanco, like Espolon
- ¼ teaspoon of chili oil

Instructions:

- In a small-sized mixing bowl, combine all of the butter ingredients & set them aside.
- Preheat your Blackstone griddle at high temperature and apply a thin layer of oil on top of the griddle.
- Cook the oysters for around 1 to 2 minutes on each side on the griddle.
- Salt flakes should be sprinkled over the oysters.
- Microwave the butter for 30 seconds, then drizzle the warm tequila butter over the oysters in plates.

Pop-Open Clams with Horseradish-Tabasco Sauce

(Preparation time: 10 minutes | Cooking time: 10 minutes | Servings: 4)

Per serving: Calories 191, Total fat 13g, Protein 15g, Carbs 4g

Ingredients:

- 2 tablespoons of horseradish, drained
- 1 tablespoon of fresh lemon juice
- 2 dozen littleneck clams, scrubbed
- Sea salt
- 1/4 teaspoon of lemon zest, finely grated
- 4 tablespoons of unsalted butter, softened
- 1 tablespoon of hot sauce, like Tabasco
- 1/4 teaspoon of smoked paprika

Instructions:

- Preheat your Blackstone griddle at high temperature and apply a thin layer of oil on top of the griddle.
- Combine the horseradish, hot sauce, paprika, lemon zest, lemon juice, & a pinch of salt in a mixing bowl.
- Cook the clams on the griddle for around 25 seconds, or till they pop open.
- Using tongs, carefully flip the clams over, so the flesh side is down.
- Cook for a further 20 seconds, or till the clam fluids begin to simmer.
- Place the clams in a serving dish and set them aside.
- Serve with roughly 1/2 teaspoon of the sauce on top of each.

Spicy Squid

(Preparation time: 10 minutes | Cooking time: 10 minutes | Servings: 4)

Per serving: Calories 292, Total fat 9g, Protein 28g, Carbs 20g

Ingredients:

- Olive oil
- 1 ½ lbs. Squid, prepared

For the marinade:

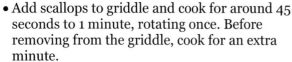

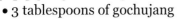

- 3 tablespoons of gochujang
- 2 teaspoons of sesame oil
- 1 teaspoon of yellow mustard
- 2 cloves of garlic cloves, minced
- 2 green onions, chopped
- ½ teaspoon of ginger, minced
- 3 tablespoons of corn syrup
- 1 teaspoon of soy sauce
- 1 teaspoon of sesame seeds

Instructions:

- Brush your Blackstone griddle using olive oil and preheat it at medium-high temperature.
- Cook the squid & tentacles for around 1 minute on the griddle, or till the bottom is firm & opaque.
- Cook for another minute on the opposite side; if the body curls, straighten it out with tongs.
- Cook for a further 2 minutes after basting with sauce on top of the squid.
- Cook for 1 minute on the opposite side, till the sauce, has evaporated and the squid has turned red and glossy.

Delicious Crab Cakes

(Preparation time: 10 minutes | Cooking time: 15 minutes | Servings: 6)

Per serving: Calories 202, Total fat 8g, Protein 13g, Carbs 17g

Ingredients:

- 1 tablespoon of parsley, chopped
- 1 egg
- 2 teaspoons of Dijon mustard
- 1 lb. of crab meat
- 1 teaspoon of lemon juice
- 1 cup of breadcrumbs
- 1/3 cup of mayonnaise
- 1 teaspoon of old bay seasoning

Instructions:

- In a mixing bowl, combine all of the ingredients and stir till well blended.
- Preheat your Blackstone griddle at medium-high temperature.

- Coat the top of the griddle using cooking spray.
- Make 6 patties with the ingredients and cook for around 6 minutes on each side on a hot griddle.
- Enjoy your meal.

Tasty Herb Fish

(Preparation time: 10 minutes | Cooking time: 10 minutes | Servings: 2)

Per serving: Calories 210, Total fat 6g, Protein 25g, Carbs 15g

Ingredients:

- 1/2 teaspoon of dried basil
- 1/8 teaspoon of salt
- 1/2 lb. of cod fillets
- 2 tablespoons of breadcrumbs
- 1 egg, lightly beaten
- 1/4 cup of Bisquick mix

Instructions:

- Place the egg in a small-sized dish.
- Mix breadcrumbs, basil, Bisquick mix, & salt in a separate shallow dish.
- Preheat your Blackstone griddle at medium-high temperature.
- Coat the top of the griddle using cooking spray.
- After dipping the fish fillets in the egg, coat them with the breadcrumb mixture.
- Cook the fish fillets for around 8-10 minutes on a heated griddle top.
- Enjoy your meal.

Game Day Recipes

- 1/2 cup of chopped scallions
- Chips, crostini or vegetables for serving
- 1 Pound of cream cheese, softened
- 1 cup of shredded cheddar cheese
- 8 slices of bacon, cooked and chopped
- 1/2 cup of shredded Parmesan cheese

For the topping:

- 1/2 cup of shredded Parmesan cheese
- 1 cup of panko breadcrumbs
- 1/4 cup of butter, melted

Instructions:

- Preheat your Blackstone griddle at 350°F.
- Combine cream cheese & mayonnaise in the dish of a stand mixer and beat with paddle attachment till smooth. Combine the rest of the ingredients for the dip in a mixing bowl.
- Smooth the top of the dip in a cast-iron skillet. To make the topping, combine all of the ingredients & put it on top of your dip. Cook for around 20 to 30 minutes on the griddle, or till the top is gently browned, and the dip is bubbling on the griddle.
- Serve with crostini, dipping chips, or vegetables. Enjoy!

Game Day Cheese Dip

(Preparation time: 10 minutes | Cooking time: 20 minutes | Servings: 6)

Per serving: Calories 311, Total fat 18g, Protein 25g, Carbs 4g

Ingredients:

- 8 ounces of cream cheese, softened
- 2 cups of Swiss cheese
- 1/2 cup of smoked almonds
- 8 slices of crumbled cooked bacon
- 1/2 cup of mayonnaise
- 2 teaspoons of fresh horseradish
- 2 teaspoons of Dijon mustard
- Crackers or vegetables, for serving
- 5 whole scallions, chopped

Instructions:

- Preheat your Blackstone griddle at 400°F.

Ultimate Game Day Dip

(Preparation time: 10 minutes | Cooking time: 30 minutes | Servings: 6)

Per serving: Calories 78, Total fat 4g, Protein 7g, Carbs 2g

Ingredients:

- 1 cup of mayonnaise
- 6 jalapeños, seeded, ribs removed & finely diced

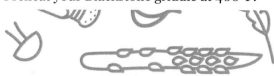

- Mix the Dijon mustard, cream cheese, mayonnaise, crumbled bacon, 1 1/2 cups of Swiss cheese, 4 sliced scallions, horseradish, and almonds together in a medium-sized mixing dish.
- Fill a small shallow casserole halfway with water. Finish with the remaining 1/4 cup of Swiss cheese on top of the dip.
- On the griddle, place the casserole dish. Cook, covered, for around 15-18 minutes, or till golden and bubbling around the edges.
- Remove the cheese dip out from the griddle and top with the chopped scallions that have been set aside. As preferred, serve with the crackers or cut vegetables. Enjoy!

Mandarin Wings

(Preparation time: 10 minutes | Cooking time: 30 minutes | Servings: 2)

Per serving: Calories 207, Total fat 7g, Protein 28g, Carbs 7g

Ingredients:

- Chicken Rub
- 1 bottle (12 oz.) of mandarin orange sauce
- 2 pounds of chicken wings, flats & drumettes separated
- Beef Rub

Instructions:

- Using mandarin sauce, coat the chicken wings. Rub the wings using Beef Rub & Chicken Rub. Allow for at least 30 minutes of marinating time.
- Preheat your Blackstone griddle at 350°F and apply a thin layer of oil on top of the griddle.
- Cook the wings for around 30 minutes on the griddle. Enjoy!

Chimichurri Sauce

(Preparation time: 5 minutes | Cooking time: 10 minutes | Servings: 4)

Per serving: Calories 145, Total fat 14g, Protein 1g, Carbs 6g

Ingredients:

- 4 cloves of garlic, diced
- 1/2 teaspoon of black pepper
- 2 whole lemons, halved
- 1 teaspoon of salt
- 2 medium flat-leaf Italian parsley, washed & chopped with the majority of stems cut off
- 1/4 cup of red wine vinegar
- 1/4 cup of extra-virgin olive oil

Instructions:

- Preheat your Blackstone griddle at 450°F and apply a thin layer of oil on top of the griddle.
- Cook for around 5 minutes, or till charred, by placing the lemon halves on the griddle.
- Remove the lemons from the griddle and squeeze them. In a food processor, combine all of the ingredients and puree till smooth, or leave somewhat lumpy for texture.
- If you like a milder flavor, add more olive oil to taste. Serve as a side dish or a dip.

Buffalo Chicken Dip

(Preparation time: 10 minutes | Cooking time: 30 minutes | Servings: 6)

Per serving: Calories 246, Total fat 21g, Protein 11g, Carbs 2g

Ingredients:

- 1 teaspoon of kosher salt
- 1 cup of cream cheese, softened
- 1 cup of shredded mozzarella cheese
- 1/2 cup of mayonnaise
- 2 cups of cooked chicken, shredded
- 4 strips of cooked bacon, crumbled
- 1/2 cup of mayonnaise
- 1 cup of shredded cheddar cheese
- 1/2 cup of sour cream
- 2 tablespoons of dry ranch seasoning
- 1/2 cup of RedHot Sauce
- Chips, crostini, crackers, or sliced vegetables for serving
- 1/2 cup of blue cheese

Instructions:

- Preheat your Blackstone griddle at 350°F.
- Combine cream cheese, salt, sour cream, mayonnaise, ranch dressing, & spicy sauce in a medium-sized mixing dish or the bowl of the stand mixer.
- Combine the cheddar, mozzarella, & shredded chicken. Move to an ovenproof dish & cover with crumbled bacon and blue cheese.
- Cook for around 20 to 30 minutes, till the top is golden brown & the dip is bubbling directly on the griddle.
- Serve with crostini, chips, crackers, or veggies sliced thinly. Enjoy!

Peanut Butter Bars

(Preparation time: 15 minutes | Cooking time: 25 minutes | Servings: 5)

Per serving: Calories 588, Total fat 28g, Protein 12g, Carbs 30g

Ingredients:

- 3/4 cup of sugar
- 1/3 teaspoon of salt
- 1 1/2 teaspoons of vanilla extract
- 1 1/2 cups of quick oats
- 3/4 cup of butter softened
- 3/4 teaspoon of baking soda
- 3/4 cup of brown sugar
- 2 eggs
- 1 1/2 cups of all-purpose flour
- 3/4 cup of peanut butter
- 2 cups of chocolate chips

For the Frosting:

- 3/4 cup of peanut butter
- 1 cup of powdered sugar
- Milk to the desired consistency

Instructions:

Preheat your Blackstone griddle at 350°F.

- In a medium-sized mixing bowl, cream together the butter & sugars till light and fluffy. Stir in the eggs one at a time, then add the peanut butter & vanilla, mixing thoroughly after each addition. Combine the flour, baking soda, and salt in a mixing bowl, then stir in the oats.
- Cook for around 10-12 minutes after spreading onto a baking sheet.
- In a medium-sized mixing bowl, combine the frosting ingredients while the bars are baking. Set them aside.
- Distribute chocolate chips evenly on top of the peanut butter bars as soon as they come out of the griddle. Wait a few minutes for them to melt, then spread them out evenly.
- Spread icing evenly over the top of the peanut butter bars once they have finished cooling.

Honey Sriracha Chex Mix

(Preparation time: 15 minutes | Cooking time: 1-hour | Servings: 4)

Per serving: Calories 314, Total fat 35g, Protein 26g, Carbs 42g

Ingredients:

- 2 cups of roasted peanuts
- 1/4 cup of sriracha sauce
- 6 cups of corn chex
- 1 cup of bag popcorn
- 1/4 cup of honey
- 6 cups of rice chex
- 1 cup of pretzels
- 4 tablespoons of butter

Instructions:

- Preheat your Blackstone griddle at 350°F. Combine all dry ingredients in a large-sized mixing dish.
- Melt butter in a large-sized roasting pan or Dutch oven on the griddle, then add Sriracha & honey.
- Gradually drizzle in the cereal mixture till it is evenly coated.
- Cook for around 1 hour, tossing every 15 minutes. To cool, spread on the parchment paper.
- Keep it in an airtight container.

Brisket Sandwich

(Preparation time: 15 minutes | Cooking time: 15 minutes | Servings: 4)

Per serving: Calories 452, Total fat 32g, Protein 18g, Carbs 22g

Ingredients:

- 2 jalapenos, thinly sliced
- 2 tablespoons of olive oil
- 4 brioche buns
- 12 to 15 slices of leftover brisket
- Salt & pepper to taste
- 1 sliced white onion
- 4 to 8 extra sharp cheddar cheese, sliced
- 2 tablespoons of butter

Instructions:

- Preheat your Blackstone griddle at 350°F.
- Preheat a cast-iron pan on the griddle. Combine the olive oil & butter. Add onions, salt, & pepper after the butter has melted. Cook onions till golden brown and soft. Mix together the jalapenos with the onions. Allow 3-4 minutes for the jalapenos to fry. Place the cheese slices on top & allow to melt.
- Cook the buns to make them toasty on the griddle. When the buns are toasted, top with sliced brisket, onion, jalapenos, & cheese.
- Serve with a dipping sauce of your choice.

Fried Cheese Curds

(Preparation time: 15 minutes | Cooking time: 15 minutes | Servings: 4)

Per serving: Calories 370, Total fat 31g, Protein 16g, Carbs 7g

Ingredients:

- 1/4 cup of milk
- 1 cup of all-purpose flour
- 2 lbs. of cheese curds
- 1 can of beer
- 2-quarts of corn oil
- 2 large eggs

Instructions:

- Preheat your Blackstone griddle at 350°F.
- In a deep Dutch oven, heat the corn oil on the griddle.
- Whisk together the milk, beer, flour, and eggs in a large-sized mixing dish till smooth. 6-10 cheese curds should be coated in batter. Remove the extra batter using a wire strainer & shake it off. Place the covered cheese curds in the hot oil and cook till golden brown, about 1-2 minutes.
- Drain on a platter lined using paper towels. As needed, repeat the process. Serve immediately.

Bloomin Onion Bites

(Preparation time: 15 minutes | Cooking time: 25 minutes | Servings: 6)

Per serving: Calories 47, Total fat 2g, Protein 2g, Carbs 6g

Ingredients:

For the Onion Bites:

- 1-pint of buttermilk
- 1 tablespoon of pepper
- 1 tablespoon of paprika
- 2 bags of pearl onions
- Vegetable oil for frying
- 1 tablespoon of kosher salt
- 2 eggs
- 1 teaspoon of cayenne pepper
- 2 cups of all-purpose flour

For the Dip:

- 1/4 cup of sour cream
- 1/2 teaspoon of paprika
- 1/4 cup of mayonnaise
- Pinch of salt & pepper
- 1 tablespoon of ketchup

Instructions:

- Preheat your Blackstone griddle at 350°F.
- Combine the eggs & buttermilk in a mixing bowl. To make four portions, peel the onions, cut off their root, and make two slices 3/4 of the way down from the root to the tip. Allow 30

minutes for the onions to soak in the buttermilk egg mixture.

- Heat the oil in the fry pot on the griddle.
- Combine flour, salt, paprika, pepper, & cayenne pepper. Roll the onions in the flour mixture, making sure to get flour between the layers & portions. Fry onions till golden brown.

Appetizer Recipes

- Preheat your Blackstone griddle at a medium-high temperature and apply a thin layer of oil on top of the griddle.
- Cook the mushroom skewers for around 2-3 minutes on each side on a hot griddle.
- Serve.

Balsamic Mushroom Skewers

(Preparation time: 10 minutes | Cooking time: 10 minutes | Servings: 4)

Per serving: Calories 60, Total fat 1g, Protein 6g, Carbs 8g

Ingredients:

- 1/2 teaspoon of chopped thyme
- 2 tablespoons of Balsamic vinegar
- 2 lbs. of sliced ¼-inch thick Mushrooms
- 1 tablespoon of soy sauce
- Pepper & salt to taste
- 3 chopped garlic cloves

Instructions:

- Combine the mushrooms and the remaining ingredients in a mixing dish, cover, and chill for around 30 minutes.
- Using skewers, thread marinated mushrooms.

Sweet Potato Fries

(Preparation time: 10 minutes | Cooking time: 15 minutes | Servings: 4)

Per serving: Calories 230, Total fat 6g, Protein 4g, Carbs 40g

Ingredients:

- 2 tablespoons of olive oil
- 2 lbs. peeled & cut into ½-inch wedges Sweet potatoes
- Pepper & salt to taste

Instructions:

- Preheat your Blackstone griddle at a medium-high temperature and apply a thin layer of oil on top of the layer.
- Toss sweet potatoes using oil, pepper, & salt in a large-sized mixing bowl.
- Cook sweet potato wedges for around 6 minutes on a heated griddle.
- Cook for another 6-8 minutes on the other side.
- Serve and enjoy.

Southwest Chicken Drumsticks

(Preparation time: 10 minutes | Cooking time: 30 minutes | Servings: 8)

Per serving: Calories 165, Total fat 12g, Protein 10g, Carbs 2g

Ingredients:

- 2 tablespoons of taco seasoning
- 2 lbs. of chicken legs
- 2 tablespoons of olive oil

Instructions:

- Preheat your Blackstone griddle at medium-high temperature and apply a thin layer of oil on top of the griddle.
- Brush the oil on the chicken legs and season them using taco seasoning.
- Cook for around 30 minutes on a hot griddle with chicken legs.
- After every 10 minutes, turn the chicken legs.
- Serve.

Curried Cauliflower Skewers

(Preparation time: 10 minutes | Cooking time: 15 minutes | Servings: 6)

Per serving: Calories 100, Total fat 8g, Protein 1g, Carbs 6g

Ingredients:

- 1 cut into wedges onion
- 1/4 cup of olive oil
- 3 teaspoons of curry powder
- 1 cut into florets large cauliflower head
- 1/2 teaspoon of ground ginger
- 1 cut into squares yellow bell pepper
- 1/2 teaspoon of salt
- 1 fresh lemon juice
- 1/2 teaspoon of garlic powder

Instructions:

- Whisk together the oil, lemon juice, curry powder, garlic, ginger, & salt in a large-sized mixing dish. Toss in the cauliflower florets till evenly coated.
- Preheat your Blackstone griddle at medium-high temperature and apply a thin layer of oil on top of the griddle.
- Using skewers, thread the cauliflower florets, onion, & bell pepper.
- Cook the skewers for around 6-7 minutes on each side on a hot griddle.
- Serve.

Griddle Potato Skewers

(Preparation time: 10 minutes | Cooking time: 25 minutes | Servings: 8)

Per serving: Calories 135, Total fat 5g, Protein 2g, Carbs 20g

Ingredients:

- 2 teaspoons of crushed dried rosemary
- 1/2 cup of mayonnaise
- 2 lbs. of quartered Potatoes
- 1/2 cup of water
- 1 teaspoon of garlic powder
- 4 tablespoons of dry white wine

Instructions:

- In a microwave-safe bowl, combine potatoes and water and simmer for around 15 minutes, or till potatoes are cooked.
- Drain the potatoes thoroughly and set them aside to cool. Combine mayonnaise, rosemary, garlic powder, & wine in a large-sized mixing dish.
- Toss in the potatoes to coat. Refrigerate for 1 hour after covering the bowl.
- Preheat your Blackstone griddle at high and apply a thin layer of oil on top of the griddle. Remove the potatoes out from the marinade and skewer them.
- Cook for around 6-8 minutes on a hot griddle with potato skewers. Halfway through, turn the skewers.
- Serve.

Parmesan Tomatoes

(Preparation time: 10 minutes | Cooking time: 20 minutes | Servings: 6)

Per serving: Calories 130, Total fat 8g, Protein 6g, Carbs 9g

Ingredients:

- 1/2 teaspoon of ground black pepper
- 1 tablespoon of dried rosemary
- 9 halved tomatoes
- 5 minced garlic cloves
- 1 cup of grated Parmesan cheese
- 1/4 teaspoon of onion powder
- 1 teaspoon of kosher salt
- 2 tablespoons of olive oil

Instructions:

- Preheat your Blackstone griddle at medium temperature and apply a thin layer of oil on top of the griddle.
- Cook for around 5-7 minutes with the sliced side of the tomatoes down on the griddle.
- In a medium-sized pan, heat the olive oil on the griddle. Cook for around 3-5 minutes with the garlic, onion powder, rosemary, black pepper, and salt.
- Remove the pan from the griddle and set it aside. Brush each tomato half with the olive oil garlic combination & sprinkle with grated parmesan cheese before serving.
- Close the griddle and continue to cook for another 7-10 minutes, or till the cheese has melted.
- Remove the tomatoes from the griddle & serve immediately.

Tasty Bread Pizza

(Preparation time: 10 minutes | Cooking time: 10 minutes | Servings: 4)

Per serving: Calories 71, Total fat 2g, Protein 3g, Carbs 11g

Ingredients:

- 4 bread slices
For the toppings:

- 1/2 cup of bell pepper, cubed
- 1/2 teaspoon of oregano
- 10 olives, sliced
- 2 tablespoons of pizza sauce
- 1 onion, cubed
- 1/2 cup of mozzarella cheese, grated
- 1 small tomato, cubed
- 1/4 teaspoon of red chili flakes

Instructions:

- Pizza sauce should be spread on the bread slices. Olives, tomatoes, bell pepper, & onion go on top.
- Chili flakes, oregano, & cheese are sprinkled on top.
- Preheat your Blackstone griddle at medium-high temperature.

- Place the bread slices on the hot griddle top, cover, and cook till the cheese melts.
- Enjoy your meal.

Corn Cakes

(Preparation time: 10 minutes | Cooking time: 10 minutes | Servings: 10)

Per serving: Calories 122, Total fat 4g, Protein 6g, Carbs 16g

Ingredients:

- 1/2 teaspoon of pepper
- 1/2 cup of cheddar cheese, shredded
- 4 eggs
- 1 jalapeno, chopped
- 1/2 cup of cornmeal
- 2 cups of corn
- 1/2 teaspoon of kosher salt
- 1/2 cup of flour
- 2/3 cup of green onions, sliced

Instructions:

- Place the corn in a food processor and pulse till it is coarsely chopped.
- Mix the corn with the remaining ingredients in a mixing dish till everything is well blended.
- Preheat your Blackstone griddle at medium-high.
- Coat the top of the griddle using cooking spray.
- Make patties out of the mixture and fry on a hot griddle till golden brown on both sides.
- Enjoy your meal.

Tortilla Pizza

(Preparation time: 10 minutes | Cooking time: 10 minutes | Servings: 1)

Per serving: Calories 336, Total fat 16g, Protein 26g, Carbs 15g

Ingredients:

- 1 tortilla
For the topping:

- 1/2 teaspoon of garlic, minced
- 3 tablespoons of mozzarella cheese, shredded
- 1/4 teaspoon of red chili flakes
- 2 teaspoons of onion, chopped
- 1/4 teaspoon of dried oregano
- 1/4 cup of tomatoes, chopped
- Salt & pepper to taste

Instructions:

- To make a tortilla, combine tomatoes, onion, pepper, garlic, oregano, chili flakes, cheese, and salt.
- Preheat your Blackstone griddle at medium-high.
- Coat the top of the griddle using cooking spray.
- Cover and heat the tortilla on a hot griddle till cheese melts.
- Enjoy your meal.

Tomato Avocado Bruschetta

(Preparation time: 10 minutes | Cooking time: 10 minutes | Servings: 6)

Per serving: Calories 142, Total fat 12g, Protein 2g, Carbs 10g

-

Ingredients:

- 2 tablespoons of olive oil
- 6 bread slices

For the topping:

- 1 garlic clove, minced
- 1 avocado, peel & dice
- 1 tomato, chopped
- 1/4 teaspoon of sea salt
- 1 cucumber, diced

Instructions:

- Preheat your Blackstone griddle at medium-high.
- Brush bread slices using oil and set on a heated griddle top, cooking till both sides are softly golden brown.
- Combine all topping ingredients inside a mixing dish & stir thoroughly.

- Using a spoon, spread the topping mixture over the bread slices.
- Enjoy your meal.

Chicken Pizza Sandwich

(Preparation time: 10 minutes | Cooking time: 10 minutes | Servings: 2)

Per serving: Calories 443, Total fat 28g, Protein 33g, Carbs 13g

Ingredients:

- 1 tablespoon of butter
- 4 bread slices
- 2 tablespoons of olives, sliced
- 1 chicken breast, cooked & sliced
- 8 pepperoni slices
- 4 mozzarella cheese slices
- 2 tablespoons of pizza sauce

Instructions:

- On one half of each bread slice, spread butter.
- Spread pizza sauce on two bread pieces and top with the chicken, pepperoni slices, olives, & cheese.
- Cover using the rest of the bread slices.
- Preheat your Blackstone griddle at medium-high.
- Coat the top of the griddle using cooking spray.
- Place the sandwiches on a hot griddle top & cook for around 5 minutes, or till both sides are softly golden brown.
- Enjoy your meal.

Pineapple Slices

(Preparation time: 10 minutes | Cooking time: 15 minutes | Servings: 4)

Per serving: Calories 108, Total fat 3g, Protein 2g, Carbs 21g

Ingredients:

- 1 tablespoon of butter, melted
- Salt to taste

- 4 pineapple slices
- 1/4 teaspoon of chili powder

Instructions:

- Preheat your Blackstone griddle at medium-high.
- Using butter, chili spice, & salt, brush pineapple slices.
- Cook pineapple slices for around 5-6 minutes on each side on a hot griddle top.
- Enjoy your meal.

Roasted Spicy Almonds

(Preparation time: 15 minutes | Cooking time: 30 minutes | Servings: 4)

Per serving: Calories 276, Total fat 18g, Protein 8g, Carbs 22g

Ingredients:

- 2 tablespoons of olive oil
- 2 teaspoons of sugar
- 1 pound of raw almonds
- 1 tablespoon of Cajun rub

Instructions:

- Combine the almonds and 1 tablespoon of olive oil in a mixing bowl & toss to coat the nuts. Add more oil if necessary.
- Mix the sugar & Cajun Rub together till the almonds are evenly covered. Place on a rimmed baking sheet coated using parchment paper or aluminum foil.
- Preheat your Blackstone griddle at 300°F and apply a thin layer of oil on top of the griddle.
- Roast the nuts for around 30 minutes, stirring once in a while.
- If not serving straight away, allow cooling completely before transferring to a jar using a tight-fitting lid.

Dessert Recipes

- Add the milk & melted butter to a cast iron griddle onto your griddle. Mix everything together for a minute.
- Once it's warmed up, sprinkle the chocolate chips on top, ensuring sure they're in a single layer. Arrange the marshmallows on top of the chocolate, standing them on end & coating it.
- Cover and set aside for 5 to 7 minutes to cook. The marshmallows must be lightly toasted before serving.
- Remove from the griddle serve with graham crackers and apple wedges.

Pumpkin Chocolate Chip Cookies

(Preparation time: 10 minutes | Cooking time: 15 minutes | Servings: 8)

Per serving: Calories 93, Total fat 5g, Protein 2g, Carbs 14g

Ingredients:

- 1/2 teaspoon of baking soda
- 2 cups of flour
- 1 teaspoon of baking powder
- 1 teaspoon of ground cinnamon
- ½ teaspoon of salt
- 1/2 teaspoon of pumpkin pie spice
- 1/4 teaspoon of ground nutmeg
- 1/2 cup of butter
- 1/2 teaspoon of ground ginger
- 1 cup of Pumpkin, canned
- 1 cup of sugar
- 1 egg
- 2 cups of chocolate chips
- 1 teaspoon of vanilla extract

Instructions:

- Preheat your Blackstone griddle at 350°F with the lid closed.
- All but 1 teaspoon of the pumpkin spice should be discarded.
- Whip the butter in a separate dish till light and fluffy. Combine the sugar egg, pumpkin puree, & vanilla extract.
- Gradually incorporate the dry ingredients into the wet ones. Inside them fold the chocolate chips.

S'mores Dip

(Preparation time: 10 minutes | Cooking time: 25 minutes | Servings: 8)

Per serving: Calories 217, Total fat 5g, Protein 3g, Carbs 31g

Ingredients:

- ¼ cup of milk
- Graham crackers
- 2 cups of marshmallows
- 1 1/4 cups of semisweet chocolate chips
- 2 tablespoons of melted salted butter
- Apple wedges

Instructions:

- Preheat your Blackstone griddle at 450°F with the lid closed.

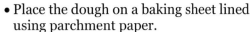

- Place the dough on a baking sheet lined using parchment paper.
- Cook for around 10 minutes, or till the cookies are lightly browned. Warm-up. Enjoy!

Mango with Lime and Coconut

(Preparation time: 10 minutes | Cooking time: 20 minutes | Servings: 2)

Per serving: Calories 115, Total fat 6g, Protein 2g, Carbs 14g

Ingredients:

- 3 tablespoons of maple syrup
- 4 whole ripe mangoes
- 1 cup of coconut flakes
- 3 tablespoons of lime zest
- 4 cups of coconut yogurt
- 1 teaspoon of chili powder

Instructions:

- Preheat your Blackstone griddle at 400°F with the lid closed.
- Apply maple syrup to the mango cheeks.
- On the griddle, golden-brown mangoes in a pan, toast the coconut flakes till light golden brown.
- In a bowl, mix together the coconut yogurt, mango, toasted coconut, lime zest, and chili powder. Enjoy!

Croissant S'mores on the Griddle

(Preparation time: 10 minutes | Cooking time: 5 minutes | Servings: 6)

Per serving: Calories 200, Total fat 11g, Protein 4g, Carbs 22g

Ingredients:

- 25 large marshmallows, regular
- 6 croissants
- 8 ounces of chocolate

Instructions:

- Preheat your Blackstone griddle at 350°F with the lid closed.
- Place them cut-side down croissant halves on the griddle & toast for around 1 minute. (Be careful since they will toast quickly.)
- Remove the first half of the croissant from the griddle and top with the second half to make a toasted croissant s'mores sandwich.
- To melt the chocolate and toast the marshmallows, place the croissant sandwiches on the griddle for around 30-60 seconds.
- Remove the s'mores from the griddle and serve them warm. Enjoy!

Caramel Bananas

(Preparation time: 15 minutes | Cooking time: 15 minutes | Servings: 4)

Per serving: Calories 152, Total fat 2g, Protein 2g, Carbs 36g

Ingredients:

- ½ cup of sweetened condensed milk
- 2 tablespoons of corn syrup
- 4 slightly green bananas
- ½ cup of butter
- 1/3 cup of chopped pecans
- ½ cup of brown sugar

Instructions:

- Preheat your Blackstone griddle at 350°F with the lid closed.
- Bring the milk, corn syrup, butter, & brown sugar to the boil in a large-sized pot on the griddle. Simmer the mixture over for five minutes. Stir the mixture constantly.
- Place the bananas on the griddle with their peels on and cook for five minutes. Cook for another five minutes on the other side. The peels will be black and prone to splitting.
- Place on a plate to serve. Remove the ends of the bananas & split the peel in half. Remove the skin from the bananas and top with caramel. Pecans should be sprinkled on top.

Apple Cobbler

(Preparation time: 20 minutes | Cooking time: 55 minutes | Servings: 8)

Per serving: Calories 152, Total fat 5g, Protein 2g, Carbs 26g

Ingredients:

- 1 cup of sugar
- 2 cups of plain flour
- 8 Granny Smith apples
- ½ cup of brown sugar
- 1 stick of melted butter
- A pinch of salt
- 2 eggs
- 1 teaspoon of cinnamon
- 2 teaspoons of baking powder
- 1 ½ cup of sugar

Instructions:

- Apples should be peeled and quartered before being placed in a bowl. Combine the cinnamon & one cup of sugar. Stir thoroughly to coat, then set aside for one hour.
- Preheat your Blackstone griddle at 350°F with the lid closed.
- Combine the salt, baking powder, sugar, eggs, brown sugar, & flour in a large-sized mixing dish. Mix till crumbs form.
- Place the apples on the rack. Drizzle the melted butter on top of the crumble mixture.
- Place on the griddle for around 50 minutes to cook.

Bacon Chocolate Chip Cookies

(Preparation time: 20 minutes | Cooking time: 30 minutes | Servings: 6)

Per serving: Calories 167, Total fat 9g, Protein 2g, Carbs 21g

Ingredients:

- 1 teaspoon of vanilla
- 1 ½ teaspoons of baking soda
- 2 ¾ cups of all-purpose flour

- 1 ½ stick of softened butter
- 8 slices cooked & crumbled bacon
- 2 room temp eggs
- ½ teaspoon of salt
- 2 ½ teaspoons of apple cider vinegar
- 1 cup of light brown sugar
- 2 cups of semisweet chocolate chips
- 1 cup of granulated sugar

Instructions:

- Combine the salt, baking soda, and flour in a mixing bowl.
- Cream together the sugar and butter in a mixing bowl. Reduce the pace. Combine the eggs, vinegar, & vanilla extract.
- Slowly stir in the flour mixture, bacon pieces, & chocolate chips over a moderate.
- Preheat your Blackstone griddle at 375°F with the lid closed.
- Place a sheet of parchment paper on a baking sheet and drop a teaspoon of cookie batter onto the sheet. Allow them to cook for about 12 minutes on the griddle, covered, or till browned.

Bourbon Monkey Bread

(Preparation time: 15 minutes | Cooking time: 40 minutes | Servings: 6)

Per serving: Calories 200, Total fat 9g, Protein 3g, Carbs 28g

Ingredients:

- 1 cup of sugar
- 3 cans of Pillsbury Grands! Southern Style Buttermilk Biscuits
- 3 teaspoons of ground cinnamon
- 1 cup of butter, unsalted
- 1 tablespoon of bourbon
- 1 cup of dark brown sugar

Instructions:

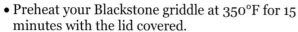

- Preheat your Blackstone griddle at 350°F for 15 minutes with the lid covered.
- Each biscuit should be divided into quarters. In a Ziploc bag, combine sugar & cinnamon, then add quartered biscuits. To coat, toss in the cinnamon sugar.
- Combine the biscuit dough and pour it into a bundt pan greased using nonstick cooking spray.
- In a small-sized saucepan on the griddle, combine the butter, brown sugar, & bourbon. Cook till the sugar has dissolved.
- Pour the butter mixture over the biscuits in the bundt pan.
- Cook in the center of the griddle for around 40 minutes, or till dark golden brown.
- Allow it to cool on the counter for around 5-10 minutes before putting it out onto a serving plate. Enjoy!

Caramelized Bourbon Pears

(Preparation time: 10 minutes | Cooking time: 30 minutes | Servings: 4)

Per serving: Calories 135, Total fat 6g, Protein 10g, Carbs 22g

Ingredients:

- 1/4 cup of brown sugar
- 3 whole slices of ripe pears,
- 1/4 cup of bourbon
- 1 teaspoon of vanilla extract
- 2 tablespoons of butter, melted
- 1/2 teaspoons of salt

Instructions:

- Preheat your Blackstone griddle at 325°F with the lid closed.
- Pears must be peeled & cored. Butter a baking dish and place them in it.
- In a small-sized mixing bowl, combine the brown sugar, butter, bourbon, vanilla, cinnamon, & salt. Pour the bourbon mixture over the pears.
- Place the baking dish on the griddle, close the lid, and cook for around 30-35 minutes, or till the pears are fork-tender.

- Drizzle the caramelized bourbon mixture all over the pears on a serving plate.
- Serve heated over vanilla ice cream. Enjoy!

Pumpkin Pie

(Preparation time: 10 minutes | Cooking time: 50 minutes | Servings: 6)

Per serving: Calories 240, Total fat 12g, Protein 3g, Carbs 29g

Ingredients:

- 15 ounces of pumpkin puree
- 4 ounces of cream cheese
- 1/3 cup of cream, whipping
- 1 teaspoon of pumpkin pie spice
- 1/2 cup of brown sugar
- 1 frozen pie crust, thawed
- 3 large eggs

Instructions:

- Preheat your Blackstone griddle at 325°F with the lid closed.
- In a mixing bowl, combine cream cheese, milk, puree, sugar, & spice. One at a time beat an egg into the mixture. Half-fill the pie crust with the ingredients.
- Cook for around 50 minutes, or till the edges are brown & the pie is hard around the edges but moves slightly in the center. Allow for thorough cooling before adding the whipped cream. Serve and enjoy yourself!

Brownie Bread Pudding

(Preparation time: 10 minutes | Cooking time: 30 minutes | Servings: 4)

Per serving: Calories 300, Total fat 14g, Protein 4g, Carbs 44g

Ingredients:

- 3 teaspoons of vanilla extract
- 4 eggs
- 1 pinch of salt
- 4 cups of Leftover brownies, cut into 1" cubes

- 1/2 cup of bittersweet chocolate chips
- 1 cup of heavy cream
- 1/4 cup of dried coconut flakes
- 1/2 cup of sugar
- 2 sticks of butter
- 1/2 teaspoon of salt
- 2 cups of brown sugar
- 1 teaspoon of baking soda
- 1/4 candied walnuts or pecans
- whipped cream

Instructions:

- Preheat your Blackstone griddle at 350°F and cover for 15 minutes.
- Combine heavy cream, eggs, sugar, vanilla, & salt in a small-sized bowl. Make a thorough mix. Combine brownies and chips in a mixing bowl.
- In a greased 9 by 13 baking pan, sprinkle coconut flakes on top.
- Cook for around 45 minutes, or till the edges are lightly browned and puffy, and the center is just set.
- In a medium-sized saucepan on the griddle, melt the butter, salt, and sugar.
- Then cook till an instant-read thermometer reads 275°F. Remove the pan from the griddle and stir in the vanilla and baking soda. It is recommended that you use caution because it may boil & steam.
- Brownie bread pudding is topped with sweetened whipped cream and candied walnuts. Enjoy!

Chewy Peanut Butter Cookies

(Preparation time: 10 minutes | Cooking time: 25 minutes | Servings: 24)

Per serving: Calories 240, Total fat 12g, Protein 5g, Carbs 27g

Ingredients:

- 1 egg whole
- 1 cup of peanut butter
- 1 cup of sugar

Instructions:

- Preheat your Blackstone griddle at 450°F with a lid covered.
- In a mixing dish, combine all of the ingredients. Place dough portions on a preheated baking sheet and cook for around 15 to 20 minutes. Allow 5 minutes for cookies to cool on the baking pan before eating!

Chocolate Chip Mint Cookies

(Preparation time: 10 minutes | Cooking time: 20 minutes | Servings: 24)

Per serving: Calories 119, Total fat 6g, Protein 2g, Carbs 16g

Ingredients:

- 1/2 teaspoon of mint extract
- 1 package of chocolate chip cookie mixture
- 8 to 10 drops of food coloring
- 1/2 cup of melted butter

Instructions:

- Preheat your Blackstone griddle at 350°F with the lid closed.
- Mix the mint essence and green food coloring into the chocolate cookie dough and bake according to the directions on the back of the box. Combine everything till it's completely smooth.
- Drop dough balls onto a parchment-lined baking sheet with a diameter of about 2 tablespoons.
- Cook for around 10 to 12 minutes on the griddle. Remove from the griddle and set aside to cool for a few minutes. Enjoy!

Plums with Balsamic Reduction

(Preparation time: 5 minutes | Cooking time: 15 minutes | Servings: 4)

Per serving: Calories 45, Total fat 2g, Protein 1g, Carbs 11g

Ingredients:

- 1/2 cup of balsamic vinegar

- 1/2 cup of brown sugar
- 10 whole smoked plums for garnishing

Instructions:

- Split the plums in half and take out the pits after cleaning them.
- Preheat your Blackstone griddle (about 400°F) for around 15 minutes.
- Cook the plums on the griddle cut-side down for around 10 minutes.
- Meanwhile, reduce the balsamic vinegar by gently simmering it with the brown sugar in a saucepan on the other side of the griddle for around 5-10 minutes, or till it has thickened and significantly reduced.
- After rotating and covering the plums with the balsamic and brown sugar reduction, cook for another 2 to 5 minutes. Plums may soften somewhat yet remain firm.
- Drizzle any leftover balsamic reduction over the plums and serve warm. Enjoy.

Seasonal Fruit with Gelato

(Preparation time: 5 minutes | Cooking time: 10 minutes | Servings: 2)

Per serving: Calories 70, Total fat 2g, Protein 1g, Carbs 18g

Ingredients:

- 1/4 cup of honey
- 3 tablespoons of turbinado sugar
- Your preferred gelato for serving
- 2 whole seasonal fruits: apricots, plums or peaches

Instructions:

- Before cooking, preheat your Blackstone griddle at 400°F and cover for around 15 minutes.
- Remove the pit from each apple before slicing it in half. Sugar should be placed on top, and honey should be sprayed on the cutting side.
- Cook the fruit with the trim side down on the griddle till charred.

- Remove the fruits from the griddle and serve with a scoop of gelato right away. If desired, drizzle with honey. Enjoy!

Buttery Chocolate with Graham Crackers

(Preparation time: 10 minutes | Cooking time: 15 minutes | Servings: 6)

Per serving: Calories 130, Total fat 3g, Protein 2g, Carbs 24g

Ingredients:

- 1/4 cup of milk
- 2 tablespoons of salted butter, melted
- 12 ounces of semisweet chocolate chips
- Graham crackers and apple wedges for serving
- 16 ounces of Jet-Puffed marshmallows

Instructions:

- Preheat your Blackstone griddle at 400°F.
- Place a cast-iron pan on the griddle and pour the melted butter and milk inside, stirring for around 1 minute.
- Sprinkle an equal amount of chocolate chips on top after the mixture starts to heat, then arrange the marshmallows standing up to completely cover the chocolate.
- Cook for around 5–7 minutes, or till marshmallows are lightly toasted.
- Remove from the griddle and serve immediately with graham crackers and apple wedges for dipping.

Dutch Baby

(Preparation time: 10 minutes | Cooking time: 30 minutes | Servings: 6)

Per serving: Calories 400, Total fat 23g, Protein 17g, Carbs 22g

Ingredients:

- 4 eggs
- 3/4 cup of all-purpose flour
- 3/4 cup of milk

- 1 egg yolk
- 1/8 teaspoon of ground nutmeg
- 1 1/2 tablespoon of sugar
- 4 tablespoons of butter
- 1 teaspoon of vanilla extract
- Powdered sugar
- Fruit, Fresh

Instructions:

- Preheat your Blackstone griddle at 400°F for around 15 minutes with the lid closed.
- Combine the eggs, flour, sugar, milk, nutmeg, & vanilla in a mixing bowl. Blend thoroughly.
- In a heated Dutch oven on the griddle, melt the butter. As soon as the butter has melted, pour in the batter (careful not to burn it).
- Cook for around 20 minutes, or till puffed and golden brown.
- Reduce the temperature of the griddle at 300°F and cook for around 5 minutes. Take the pancakes from the griddle and slice them.
- Serve with syrup, preserves, fruit, powdered sugar, & cinnamon sugar as soon as possible. Enjoy!

Pound Cake with Sour Cherry Syrup

(Preparation time: 10 minutes | Cooking time: 20 minutes | Servings: 12)

Per serving: Calories 391, Total fat 14g, Protein 6g, Carbs 42g

Ingredients:

- 4 tablespoons of sea salt
- ½ teaspoon of fresh lemon juice
1⅓ lbs. of fresh cherries

- 2 tablespoons of brown sugar, packed
- ¾ cup of sugar
- 1 cup of sour cream
- 1 pound of cake, cut into 8 slices

Instructions:

- Preheat your Blackstone griddle at medium temperature.

- In a medium-sized saucepan on the griddle, bring the cherries, sugar, 1/4 cup of water, & salt to the boil.
- Cook, stirring periodically, for around 10 minutes, till a syrup develops. Allow cooling.
- In a small-sized mixing bowl, combine sour cream, brown sugar, & lemon juice; chill till ready to serve.
- Cook for around 1 minute on each side of the pound cake on the griddle.
- Place a dollop of sour cream mixture & 1/3 cup cherry syrup on each slice of pound cake and serve.

Watermelon with Yogurt

(Preparation time: 10 minutes | Cooking time: 10 minutes | Servings: 6)

Per serving: Calories 126, Total fat 3g, Protein 5g, Carbs 22g

Ingredients:

- 1 tablespoon of white wine vinegar
- 1 cup of plain Greek yogurt
- 1/4 cup of small mint leaves
- 2 tablespoons of lemon juice
- 1 tablespoon of extra-virgin olive oil, plus more for the drizzling
- Sea salt for seasoning
- 1 teaspoon of coarsely chopped thyme
- Honey, for drizzling
- Twelve 3-inch-long triangles of the seedless red watermelon, around 1-inch thick

Instructions:

- Preheat your Blackstone griddle at a high temperature.
- In a small-sized mixing dish, combine the yogurt, thyme, lemon juice, vinegar, & 1 tablespoon of olive oil.
- Season the watermelon triangles using salt and drizzle with olive oil.

- Cook for around 1 minute on each side till charred; transfer to plates.
- Season the watermelon using black pepper and a dollop of yogurt sauce.
- To serve, garnish with mint as well as a drizzle of honey.

Mint Julep Peaches

(Preparation time: 10 minutes | Cooking time: 10 minutes | Servings: 4)

Per serving: Calories 361, Total fat 36g, Protein 5g, Carbs 20g

Ingredients:

- ½ cup of shortening
- 2 cups of packed dark brown sugar
- 4 ripe peaches
- 2 cups of vanilla bean ice cream
- ½ cup of Kentucky Bourbon
- 4 stems separated sprigs mint

Instructions:

- Preheat your Blackstone griddle at medium-high temperature.
- In a small-sized saucepan on the griddle, combine the bourbon, brown sugar, & mint stems. Allow 5 minutes for the sauce to reduce.
- Remove the stones from the peaches and cut them in half.
- The shortening should be applied uniformly to the flesh.
- Peaches should be cooked for around 2 minutes with the shortening side down and tented using foil.
- Rotate them at 180 degrees and cook for another 2 minutes, covered.
- Drizzle glaze over the peaches, flesh side up. Serve with ice cream & fresh mint leaves on top.

Conclusion

You make it to the end, which is fantastic. If you enjoy a hearty breakfast to start your day, you should consider purchasing an outdoor gas griddle. These plates are fantastic because they allow you to cook at low temperatures without risking flare-ups or burns. They also have safety features that automatically shut off when they sense overheating, so you don't have to worry about unintentional fires when cooking for a large group.

A good outdoor gas Griddle is a fantastic tool that will make life easier and less stressful for you. Griddles can come in handy whether you're cooking for family or friends. Everything from eggs and pancakes to grilled sandwiches & burgers may be cooked on one griddle!

When you get a good Griddle it will be a multifunctional appliance for many years to come because it is made of industrial quality materials. Pay attention to have a griddle's structure made of super-durable powder-coated steel.

If you get a good size it will be enough to cook all of the components of a whole meal simultaneously, it's ideal for families who enjoy flawlessly prepared backyard classics like burgers, steaks, and vegetables, as well as substantial breakfasts. Make everyone's eggs, bacon, hash browns, & pancakes simultaneously.

Additionally,

- Great ff you enjoy camping cooking but despise the mess.
- You'll like having all of the greases in one place for simple disposal.
- Best of all, adding this grill to your camping gear collection or hosting family and friend's gatherings won't break the budget!
- In the morning, wake up the family with eggs and bacon.
- In the evenings, ensure sure those delectable burgers are properly cooked.
- You'll never prepare a meal the same way again!

After explaining what a Griddle is, how to use, care for, and clean it, we've provided loads of tasty recipes to satisfy your taste buds. Good luck!

Made in United States
North Haven, CT
17 July 2022